ALEC JUDD

Love is the key

DayOne

© Day One Publications 2005
First printed 2005

ISBN 1 903087 79-1

9 781903 087794

Unless otherwise stated, all Scripture quotations are from the
New International Version copyright © 1973, 1978, 1984

British Library Cataloguing in Publication Data available

Published by Day One Publications
Ryelands Road, Leominster, HR6 8NZ
☎ 01568 613 740 FAX 01568 611 473
email—sales@dayone.co.uk
web site—www.dayone.co.uk
North American—e-mail—sales@dayonebookstore.com
North American—web site—www.dayonebookstore.com

Designed by Steve Devane and printed by Gutenberg Press, Malta

Dedication

With gratitude to my wife
with whom I have shared
the most loving relationship
for nearly 50 years

Contents

One of the reasons we experience conflict so acutely within the Church is that everything hinges upon relationships. Conflict is inevitable as people interact with one another.

We were made in the image of God and for relationships with each another, but sin has marred, distorted, and damaged both. Good relationships of all kinds, however, may be therapeutic and cause a person to know healing or facilitate progress towards wholeness.

The Church should be the best therapeutic community in the world. Unlike any therapeutic community built around a psychological counsellor with his client, it is not an artificial community. It emphasises acceptance (Romans 15:7), forgiveness (Ephesians 4:32), compassion (Philippians 2:1; Colossians 3:12), and grace as an unconditional and divine love (John 13:34–35; Romans 12:9–10; 1 Corinthians 13).

Conflicts, due to fractured relationships, can immobilise a Church and disintegrate a fellowship. Pastor Judd is aware of these problems. He has pastored four Churches and has a wealth of experience in analysing, advising and counselling. He faces the fact that Biblical religion is inescapably corporate. The Old Testament is a story of people and the varied ways of God's dealings with them. This is highlighted in chapter 5, 'The Menace of Misunderstanding', which deals with conflicts and relationships between the tribes of Israel (Joshua 22).

The New Testament continues this sense of corporateness. Scripture knows nothing of solitary religion. Jesus came for the salvation of his people (Matthew 1:21). No one can be reconciled to God without being reconciled to the people of God among whom his experience of God's grace immediately sets him. Thus soteriology is indissolubly bound up with ecclesiology. Salvation and the Church go hand in hand. Pastor Judd highlights that union with Christ necessarily involves union with people. He believes that the Church is not simply a 'means of grace', useful to our growth; it is a necessary part of Christian experience to be taken with the utmost seriousness. The Church is a fellowship of the Spirit. We need to affirm our commitment to the fellowship of our local Church group and examine our attitude to fellow Christians. There is practical advice in the book, dealing with attitudes and relationships, for example, 'Handling Disagreements' and 'Mending Fences'. The cohesive element in the book is the theme of Love. 'Love's Resilience' in the opening chapter contains a pragmatic exposition of 1 Corinthians 13. Other chapters highlight 'Love's Unreaped Edges'; 'When Love Breaks Down'; 'Love's Intolerance'; 'Love's Pathway' and 'Love's Fruitfulness'. I highly recommend this book to Pastors and Church leaders and suggest that they make it available to the members of their Churches and Fellowships. This would be a worthwhile investment.

William Freel,

OCTOBER 2004

Love's resilience

Relationships have a profound effect on human experience. Some enhance and enrich life, and bring us a great deal of joy. But others spoil and impoverish it, and bring us a great deal of sadness. And even the best relationships can break down and turn happiness into heartache. Love alone can stand the pressures and strains of relationships, for it has a resilience all its own. It smoothes their path as nothing else can.

What is love?

But what is love? We must begin by defining it because so many uses of the word devalue it. Paul gives us a unique portrait of it in 1 Corinthians 13, which helps to clear away the debris of misunderstanding and misconceptions that surround it. He describes love at its best. And what a perfect model he chooses for this pen portrait! As he sketches in one delightful feature after another we begin to recognize the Lord Jesus Christ. He and he alone could have been sitting in the studio of Paul's mind.

What an attractive picture emerges! Paul says, 'Love is patient, love is kind. It does not envy, it does not boast, it is not proud. It is not rude, it is not self-seeking, it is not easily angered, it keeps no record of wrongs. Love does not delight in evil but rejoices with the truth' (vv. 4–6). We see these features of love perfectly incarnated in the life of the Lord Jesus. This kind of love has no room for the 'me first' philosophy which ravages life today. It purges out our deeply ingrained selfishness. It gives us a deep concern for the welfare of others.

One writer after another has sought to drive home the importance of love amongst God's people. It has been described as 'the badge of Christ's disciples', and 'the oxygen of the kingdom', and 'the queen of all the Christian graces', and 'the silver thread' that should run through all our conduct. D.L. Moody, the American evangelist said, 'A man may be a good doctor without loving his patients; a good lawyer without loving his clients; a good geologist without loving science; but he cannot be a good Christian without love.'

As Paul completes his portrait of love he says, 'It always protects, always trusts, always hopes, always perseveres' (v. 7). He says, 'Love never fails' (v. 8). It has the power to carry burdens, suffer hardships, and make sacrifices for the good of others.

John highlights this feature of love when he says that Jesus, 'Having loved his own who were in the world, he now showed them the full extent of his love' (John 13:1). And he did that, not just by washing their feet, but by being stretched out on a cross for their sins. What resilience! At Calvary we see a love as resilient as tungsten steel, for Christ carried the heaviest of all burdens, and suffered the greatest of all hardships, and made the greatest of all sacrifices for our salvation. He 'died for sins once for all, the righteous for the unrighteous, to bring you to God' (1 Peter 3:18). There is no resilience in all the world like the resilience of love.

Love's strength

It 'always protects', or as it could be translated, it 'bears all things' (NKJV). The Greek word could mean either, but the idea of bearing up seems the better translation here. The Amplified New Testament translates it, 'Love bears up under anything *and* everything that comes'. That fits in with Paul's use of the word elsewhere. In 1 Corinthians 9:12, the NIV translates it 'we put up with anything'. This is *love's strength*.

This use of the word, like a series of slides, displays one picture after another. It was used of a roof with no leak in it, even after severe weather. It was used of troops strongly defending a fortress. It was used of ice bearing weight without cracking. All these pictures have strength in them. Love has a stamina all its own.

Ian Macpherson, in his book, *The Punctuality of God,* has a helpful sermon on the Father in the story of the Prodigal Son. He entitles it, very strikingly, 'God—Running to Reconcile'. And in that sermon he has a true story that proves that truth is stranger than fiction. How movingly it demonstrates love's stamina!

During the first of the two great wars, that left a trail of blood across the last century, an old woman, who lived in a town in the south west of Scotland, had a son working in an armaments factory. It stood seven miles away, and one day a terrible accident occurred. A fierce explosion blasted the building and the noise of it echoed and re-echoed over a wide area. The old woman heard it and she feared lest her son should be involved in the disaster. So she gathered up her skirts and *ran* the whole seven miles without stopping; a feat that would have taxed the stamina and endurance of even a strong man! But the old woman did it, and who can doubt that it was her mothers' love that gave her the strength. Fearing that her son was in danger, she fled to his side.

No retaliation

Love can suffer without retaliation. It 'bears *all* things'. It is not embittered by reproach, or shaken by ingratitude, or provoked by rudeness. It does not pay others back in their own coin. It makes no attempt to get even. It does not harbour a spirit of revenge. How wonderfully this feature of love shines out from the life of the Lord Jesus, like the sun from a clear sky. 'When they hurled their insults at him, he did not retaliate; when he suffered, he made no threats' (1 Peter 2:23). When men hammered Jesus to the Cross, pinning him there like a butterfly to a board, he prayed, 'Father, forgive them, for they do not know what they are doing' (Luke 23:34).

Love does not hit back. It turns the other cheek, it goes the second mile, it returns good for evil. It suffers scorn and ridicule, hurt and injury, without trying to get its own back. What a difference this kind of love would make in all our relationships. But it does not fruit naturally in our hearts. Like any other exotic plant it has to be imported. It is 'the fruit of the Spirit' (Galatians 5:22). It grows in us as the Holy Spirit takes possession of us for Christ, and as we allow the flag of Christ to fly willingly and unashamedly from the masthead of our lives.

No reservation

And love serves without reservation. Here again, we see its strength. Its very nature prompts it to serve, to help, to minister, to share the burdens of others. It gives without counting the cost, and serves without heeding the sacrifice. The Lord Jesus, who was incarnate love, could say to his disciples, 'I am among you as one who serves' (Luke 22:27). He gave of himself unstintingly in the service of others.

We see this feature of love clearly portrayed in John 13. When the disciples gathered with Jesus in the upper room to celebrate the Passover, no slave stood ready to wash their feet. So after supper Jesus stripped off his robe, wrapped a towel round his waist, took a basin of water, and washed and dried his disciples' feet. The Son of God stooped to that! He did the job of the most menial slave. What an amazing act of love! We feel the impact of it even today as it reaches out to us over the centuries.

True love serves without holding back. It does not say, 'That's not my job'. It was certainly not Jesus' job to wash the disciples' feet. And love does not say, 'I'm not going to serve *him*!' Jesus washed even the feet of Judas whose greedy heart had hatched plans to betray him! Such serving love moves us deeply, and in our best moments we long to be filled with it ourselves.

A great preacher closed his sermon with an earnest appeal. He urged those who wanted to trust Christ to go to the front. About twenty people responded, among them a very well-to-do lady. She asked if she might speak. She said, 'I want you to know why I've responded to the appeal. It's not because of any word the preacher said. I stand here because of the influence of a little woman who sits before me,' and she pointed her out. She said, 'Her fingers are rough with toil; the hard work of many years has bent her back and stooped her low. She's served in my home for many years, and I've never known her to become impatient, or to speak an unkind word, or to do a dishonest deed. I know of countless little acts of unselfish love that adorn her life.

I'm ashamed to say it but I've openly sneered at her faith, and laughed at her faithfulness to God. Yet when my daughter died, it was this little woman who helped me to look beyond the grave and shed my first tear of hope. The sweetness of her life has brought me to Christ. I covet what has made her life so beautiful.

At the preacher's request the little bent woman was led forward, her eyes brimming with tears of joy. Her face just shone! He turned to the congregation and said, 'Let me introduce you to the real preacher tonight', and to her great embarrassment everybody rose to acknowledge her.

Love's confidence

It 'always trusts' which is *love's confidence*. But that seems very dangerous in a world riddled with deceit. Would it not make us very vulnerable?

Would it not leave us without defences? Would it not lay us open to all kinds of deception?

Not credulous

No, because love is not credulous. I know we say, 'love is blind' but that is just not true! Love has an insight and a discernment all its own. It always sees further than others see. We look at a couple deeply in love and we say, 'I wonder what they see in each other?' They see a good deal more than we can see! Our senses have not been sharpened by their love.

Think of a mother with her child. She can often discern a need without a word being spoken. A boy had a raging toothache. He did not tell his mother, for he feared a visit to the dentist. So as they sat opposite each other in the sitting room at home, he did his best to hide his pain. Then his mother said, 'Son, have you got toothache?' Love is not blind.

Not suspicious

It 'always trusts' not because it is credulous, but because it is not suspicious. It thinks the best, not the worst. It puts the most favourable construction on things, and makes all the allowance it can for human weakness, without betraying the truth of God. What a delightful aspect of love this is. What a difference it would make if it stamped all our relationships. It would prevent many a harsh word of criticism and save us from many a misunderstanding.

Thomas Carlyle, the famous Scottish writer, pleaded eloquently for a tempered judgement on Robert Burns, the Scottish poet. He said, 'Granted the ship comes into harbour with shrouds and tackle damaged; the pilot is blameworthy; he has not been all wise and all powerful; but to know how blameworthy, tell us first whether his voyage has been round the Globe, or only to Ramsgate and the Isle of Dogs.' That was Carlyle's way of saying that love makes allowances. True love always does. In Ephesians 4:2, Paul urges us to 'Be completely humble and gentle; be patient, bearing with one another in love.' I like J.B. Phillips' paraphrase: 'Accept life with humility and patience, making allowances for each other because you love each other.'

Love sees hidden splendours and unrealized possibilities in people. That gives it its confidence even amidst failure and sin. The first time Simon Peter stood before him, Jesus looked at him with the perceptive eyes of love, and that look mastered Simon and won his heart. And Jesus said to him, 'You are … You will be' (John 1:42). Jesus read Simon's character, seeing what he was, but also seeing what the discipline of grace could make him. And Jesus gave him a name prophetic of what he would become. 'He said, "You are Simon son of John. You will be called Cephas" (which, when translated, is Peter)' (John 1:42). Both Cephas and Peter mean 'rock' and picture the moral and spiritual strength that would one day be his. He was still Simon, impulsive and indecisive, but what an incentive his new name would be to him! It would remind him of his destiny and encourage him to achieve it.

Dr Graham Scroggie in his book, *The Love Life*, has a helpful quotation. He does not tell us where it comes from, but it paints a very graphic picture. 'Through the tired ranks of the vanquished, through the throngs of the disheartened, across the trampled fields of life strewn with wasted efforts and battered dreams, love passes, still believing all things, and in the light of that brave faith, many a man stretches out his hand for his sword, and finds it worth gripping, even though it be a broken one.' Love's confidence can lift the fallen, put fresh hope into them, and set them back on their feet.

Love's optimism

Love 'bears all things' because it 'always trusts', but what happens when love's faith is betrayed? What happens when love can find no firm ground for faith? It goes on hoping for better things, because love 'always hopes'. This is *love's optimism*, and it means much more than wishful thinking. For New Testament hope has its roots in God and his grace, and that gives it a certainty and an assurance denied to this world's hopes.

Not soured by disappointment

This means that love is not soured by disappointment. It may weep over it, but its tears will glisten with hope. As Shakespeare put it, 'Love is not love that alters when it alteration finds', for it has a constancy about it. It *will* have its disappointments for we live in an imperfect world. Sin has enmeshed all of us, and we fail far too often. But love will not be soured by these disappointments. If its confidence is shaken it will not wring its hands in despair. Love 'always hopes'. That does not mean it juggles with the evidence, or tries to persuade itself that things are other than they are. Love is a realist, but amidst the setbacks of life it joins hands with hope.

We see this optimism of love in Jesus' dealings with his wayward disciples. How often they must have disappointed him! One day they vied with one another as to who was the greatest. Again and again they failed in faith and understanding. And when the crunch came they all forsook him and fled. But Jesus loved them through it all. As Petersen paraphrases John 13:1 'He continued to love them right to the end.' He never ceased to hope for better things.

But sadly our hopes are not always realized. Before Judas betrayed him, Jesus made one last appeal to him. He gave him the special piece of bread that a host gave to one of his favourite guests. Judas took it and perhaps carried it out into the night, and every step he took he was trampling on the Saviour's love. It was Judas who failed, not Jesus.

Strong in hope

We have all had disappointments in our relationships and sometimes they have been soaked with our tears. Love alone can stand the test. It is not soured by disappointment because it is strong in hope. Even in sad and difficult circumstances, when it cannot find room for its faith, love puts its hand into the hand of hope and takes its faith forward in anticipation of better things.

We pray sometimes for unsaved relatives and friends, and prayer seems to go unanswered. We long to see them saved but instead of responding to the gospel they seem to get harder. They may even become hostile, and we can get very discouraged. Only love will keep us at the grindstone of prayer. It kept my great-uncle there for twenty years, praying that God would save me. When I told him the good news he said, 'I've been praying for you since you were in your pram!' I shall always be grateful to him for his prayers.

Sometimes in our family or in our own lives, we face a seemingly impossible situation. Perhaps our son or daughter has a failing marriage, and in spite of all our attempts to help, it threatens to disintegrate. Love will look for the faintest glimmer of hope, and keep us praying for a restored relationship. It will not accept defeat until all hope vanishes like smoke in the wind.

And what a difference a *word* of hope can make. Adam Clarke became a great theologian, but he did not do well at school. One day, a distinguished visitor came to the school, and the teacher pointed to Adam and said, 'That's the stupidest boy in the school!' How unkind! It could have scarred him for life. But before he left the school the visitor sought to undo the damage. He said, 'Never mind, you may be a great scholar some day. Don't be discouraged but try hard, and keep on trying.' The teacher said, 'Hopeless!' But the visitor poured hope into Adam's heart, and surely his word of hope inspired Adam Clarke to greater things.

Love's endurance

It 'always perseveres', which is *love's endurance*. Paul uses a military word that pictures an army withstanding an enemy attack. Here is love under strain and standing up to the strain. It has a fortitude and an endurance all its own. So in 1 Corinthians 13:8, Paul can say, 'Love never fails.' He compares it with things that will fail—prophecies, tongues and knowledge. But he says, 'Love *never* fails', and the Greek word for 'fails' means to fall to the ground like the petals of a flower. Love helps us to stand up to things.

Patient amidst people

Love keeps us patient amidst people, even difficult people. Some folk can be very trying and maybe they get on our nerves. Perhaps we find them too slow, or too quick, or too talkative, or too quiet, or too morose, or too irritating. But maybe they find us a trial too! We must not forget that. Only love with its unique endurance will help us to cope.

In Ephesians 5:2, Paul says, 'Live a life of love, just as Christ loved us.' Again and again the apostle hauls us back to Christ, for what an example *he* has set us. How patient *he* was with his wayward disciples, with the fickle multitude, and with his scheming enemies. At times he rebuked them and raked their consciences with his burning words, for there was nothing soft or flabby about his love. But oh, his patience with them! 'As Christ', says Paul. Let love in all its unselfishness be the path you tread, the atmosphere you breathe, the pattern you follow. '*Live* a life of love', says the apostle.

Patient amidst pressure

And love keeps us patient amidst pressure, when the pace of life begins to turn the screw and squeeze us like a vice. How prone we are to become impatient and irritable when things go wrong, when life proves difficult at home or at work, or when we have one of those days when everything seems to fall apart. It is not easy to stay patient in such circumstances. Things can get on top of us and we feel like lashing out at those around us. Love alone can stand the strain and tension of such days. It does not fly off the handle for it has a very long fuse. It 'always perseveres'.

But we must not confuse love's endurance with a pious, mouse-like acceptance of things. It does not turn us into doormats for everybody to wipe their feet on. It puts iron into our souls. It enables us to stand up to difficult people and difficult circumstances without lapsing into depression or even despair. It gives us wings to rise above the problems of life so that they do not get on top of us. And we shall certainly improve things if we can. Love's endurance will help us to handle things for God's glory.

George Matheson, in one of his prayers, asks that he might accept God's will: 'Not with dumb resignation but with holy joy; not only with the absence of murmur but with a song of praise.' Let us make that *our* prayer, for endurance like a coin has two sides to it. Paul puts both sides together in 1 Corinthians 13:4. He puts the negative side first—'Love is patient'—but then he turns to the positive side—'love is kind'. Love's endurance is more than stoicism, suffering without complaint. It looks for ways of being kind. Indeed, love without kindness would be as unnatural as springtime without flowers.

The Christ-mastered life

This love with its strength, its confidence, its optimism, its endurance, comes from God's heart, not our hearts. Paul describes it in Galatians 5:22 as 'the fruit of the Spirit'. To try and produce it by ourselves would be like tying apples on a tree. God must grow it in our lives by the Holy Spirit, like apples growing on a tree. It only begins to appear when the Lord Jesus controls us by his Spirit. So let us yield to the Saviour each new day. Let us put him in charge of things. Let us throw open every door in the house of our lives, especially the door of the director's room, and give Jesus the run of the house. A yielded life means no locked doors.

We love by loving

But we learn to love only by loving. In 1 Corinthians 14:1 Paul says, 'Follow the way of love', and the Greek word for 'follow' has the idea of pursuit in it, like a dog chasing a hare. Petersen's paraphrase captures the all-out effort involved: 'Go after a life of love as if your life depended on it—because it does.' The effort is ours but the enabling is his. For nobody becomes an artist just by looking at pictures, and nobody becomes a musician just by listening to music. The paints must be mixed, and the instruments must be played. And we learn to love by practising love.

In the chapters that follow, we shall see how to make love our aim, that it may permeate all our relationships. We shall see what opportunities to embrace, and what pitfalls to avoid. And may God help us to turn theory into practice.

Love's unreaped edges

Tucked away in the heart of Leviticus, the third book in the Old Testament, we find some unreaped edges that compel us in a most instructive way to think about others. They show us how practical our love should be. But many Christians find this book a daunting book to read, because it abounds with God's instructions to his people centuries ago, and at first sight they seem irrelevant.

But when we dig deeper we discover some important principles that have no sell-by date. We see God's concern for every aspect of life, and again and again he commands practical love. This love should lay its hand on Monday as well as Sunday, indeed on every day of the week. It should make deep and lasting inroads not just into our personal life, but into our home life, our church life, our social life, and our work life. And what a transforming influence it will have on all our relationships!

Leviticus 19:9–10 illustrates this very clearly. God says, 'When you reap the harvest of your land, do not reap to the very edges of your field or gather the gleanings of your harvest. Do not go over your vineyard a second time or pick up the grapes that have fallen. Leave them for the poor and the alien. I am the Lord your God'. Leviticus 23:22 renews the challenge: 'When you reap the harvest of your land, do not reap to the very edges of your field or gather the gleanings of your harvest. Leave them for the poor and the alien. I am the Lord your God.' What practical provision this made for those in need, for Israel had no Welfare State.

God's thoughtfulness

And God sets the pace, for these unreaped edges provide a window through which we can see *his* incredible love. They light up the softer side of *his* character. His heart beats with compassion for the deprived and the needy. But God has an enemy, the devil, who gives him a bad press. He pours out a constant stream of poisonous propaganda that he might turn us against God. He shows us all the suffering in the world and he says, 'How can you say that God is a God of love? If he really cared, he would do something about it!'

Oscar Wilde used to say that there was enough suffering in any lane in London to prove that a good God does not govern the world. Life certainly throws up some difficult questions, and they are not easy to answer. Why does God allow the carnage of war? Why are disease germs so prevalent? Why should a baby be born blind, or handicapped, or mentally retarded? Why should the innocent suffer? What about natural disasters like earthquakes, famines, and tornadoes? We could multiply such questions.

In one of Hugh Walpole's greatest novels, a young man cries, 'You know there can't be a God, Vanessa. In your heart you must know it. You're a wise woman. You read and think. Well, then ask yourself, how can there be a God and life be as it is? If there is one he ought to be ashamed of himself, that's all I can say!' And many people have argued like that for they, too, think that God does not care. They have been listening to the devil's propaganda, but it is all lies! Denying God's love is not the answer to the difficult questions of life; we must look elsewhere for that. For God is the God of the unreaped edges. He has a big heart of love, and he is so thoughtful. And he wants us to reflect his love in *our* relationships.

Christ's compassion

God is not indifferent to human need. We see this wonderfully mirrored in Jesus Christ. Compassion runs like a golden thread through his life and ministry. Matthew 9:36 says, 'When he saw the crowds, he had compassion on them, because they were harassed and helpless, like sheep without a shepherd.' Matthew 14:14 says, 'When Jesus landed and saw a large crowd, he had compassion on them and healed their sick.' Mark 1:41 describes how Jesus responded to a leper's cry for help. It says, 'filled with compassion', he touched him and healed him. Compassion is a deeply caring word, and this has profound implications, for Jesus Christ is God incarnate. He is 'God thrown on the screen of human history'.

One day, a little boy stood before a photograph of his absent father. Turning to his mother he said wistfully: 'I wish Father would step out of the picture.' God did just that in his Son, Jesus Christ. He stepped out of the picture at Bethlehem. In the words of John 1:14,18, 'The Word became flesh; he came to dwell among us, and we saw his glory, such glory as befits the Father's only Son, full of grace and truth ... No one has ever seen God;

but God's only Son, he who is nearest to the Father's heart, he has made him known' (NEB).

The one, true God has stepped on to the stage of human affairs in the Person of his Son. He has made himself visible to us in Jesus Christ. That refutes the devil's lie that God does not care. He has not stood aloof from us with no interest and no concern. Neither has he just stood on the touchline of our lives shouting encouragement to us, like football supporters shouting encouragement to their team. He has become personally involved with us in all our suffering and need, for Jesus came on a rescue mission. He came to deal with the world's underlying problem—our sin. And he came to deal with it atoningly on the cross, that he might restore our broken relationship with God. With crystal clarity, 1 Peter 3:18 says, 'For Christ died for sins once for all, the righteous for the unrighteous, to bring you to God.'

We cannot look at the cross and accuse God of not caring. The same love that shines from the unreaped edges, blazes with noonday brightness from the Christ of Calvary. God cared enough to send him to be our Saviour.

God's method

The unreaped edges also reveal God's method. He helps us through our relationships with one another. We are all bound up together in the bundle of life. This accounts for a great deal of suffering in the world. If one man plays the fool, those around him can suffer. If one nation breaks its word, other nations can be plunged into conflict. But it works the other way, too.

Some people say, 'Stop the world, I want to get off!' But think what we would lose if we could do that. We would escape many of the problems of life, but we would forfeit many of the advantages, too. Because we are bound up together, our lives are enriched in countless ways. We have food to eat, clothes to wear, fuel to burn, and all the benefits of modern technology. And think of the books we read, the music we enjoy, and the medical help we need at times. All these things are ours because we belong to the human race. This may bring suffering, but it brings many good things, too.

God has made us dependent on one another; the unreaped edges teach us that. This is what makes our relationships so important. God's method is to help men through men. He does not normally rain bread from heaven. He commands the 'haves' to give to the 'have-nots'. He says in Ephesians 4:28: 'He who has been stealing must steal no longer, but must work, doing something useful with his own hands, *that he may have something to share with those in need.*' Mark the principle: God has bound us up together in the bundle of life, and made life dependent on our relationships with one another.

A poor little boy who had nothing—no home, no parents, no friends—wandered into a Salvation Army meeting. He heard about the Lord Jesus, and trusted him as his Saviour. Soon afterwards somebody said to him, 'I hear you've been converted.' 'Yes, that's right.' 'Then I suppose you think God loves you?' 'Oh yes I do,' said the boy. 'Then if God loves you, why doesn't he tell somebody to look after you and care for you?' What a tough question for the lad, but he had his answer ready. 'I expect he does tell somebody, but somebody forgets.'

Man's selfishness

God made us to help and support one another, but sadly sin has turned us in on ourselves. It has twisted and warped our attitude and outlook. It has made us self-centred and self-seeking, and selfishness has ruined countless relationships. It has left a trail of devastation across the centuries and around the world. Man is often reluctant to leave unreaped edges because he wants the whole harvest for himself. Sin blinds us to the need of others. It can dry up the springs of compassion in our hearts. It can make getting seem more important than giving.

James traces the carnage of war to human selfishness. Petersen makes this clear in his helpful paraphrase of James 4:1–2: 'Where do you think all these appalling wars and quarrels come from? Do you think they just happen? Think again. They come about because you want your own way, and fight for it deep inside yourselves. You lust for what you don't have and are willing to kill to get it. You want what isn't yours and will risk violence to get your hands on it.' We say, 'Why does God allow war?' when all the time it erupts from the volcanic depths of sinful human hearts.

God's provision

The world groans under the weight of its need. Millions go to bed hungry.

But there is no failure in God's provision. In Psalm 145:15–16, David says, 'The eyes of all look to you, and you give them their food at the proper time. You open your hand and satisfy the desires of every living thing.' God has a vast population to feed, but he has provided enough for us all. I read somewhere of a science museum that displays all that we get from the earth: iron, coal, gold, silver, copper, platinum, rock salt, gas wells, oil wells, and so on. God's provision! That museum displays the whole earth as a giant bank vault. We are all 'the pensioners of Providence'!

Man's distribution

The failure lies, not in God's provision, but in man's distribution. The economists are always telling us that the food is there, but it is not always shared out properly. So while in some parts of the world people have more than enough, in other parts they are starving. Thank God for the Aid Agencies that do such sterling work to redress the balance, but so much more could be done. God has provided ample resources, but sad to say many people waste them, hoard them, or squander them, instead of sharing them.

There is no simple answer to all the need, for sin, like an octopus, reaches its tentacles into every part of our lives, and into every part of our world. Even when help is available, it does not always reach those who need it most. And some people bring about their own poverty. They have the money, but they drink or gamble it away. And they not only deprive themselves of what they need, they deprive their families as well.

We live in a sinful world, and we have all contributed our own quota of sin to it. Our lives, too, have been spoiled by selfishness. Many people look at the need and blame God for it. But the fault lies with man, not with God. He makes ample provision and commands unreaped edges, but many people turn a deaf ear to what he says. They seem to have no care or concern for others; they just live for themselves and their own families.

Practical holiness

But if we are God's people, he wants us to be different. Leviticus 19 begins with an urgent call to holiness: 'The Lord said to Moses, "Speak to the entire assembly of Israel and say to them: 'Be holy because I, the Lord your

God, am holy'."' This call, like an underground stream, keeps surfacing in both Old Testament and New. For a holy God has always wanted a holy people. 1 Peter 1:15–16 says, 'But just as he who called you is holy, so be holy in all you do; for it is written: "Be holy, because I am holy."' And God makes holiness very practical, for the call to holiness in Leviticus 19 is quickly followed by this command about unreaped edges. So holiness is not just a private love affair with God; it is serving others, it is helping others in their need.

However much selfishness ruins relationships in the world, God commands his people to live differently. In Leviticus 19:9–10, he says, 'When you reap the harvest of *your* land, you shall not wholly reap the corners of *your* field … Leave them for the poor and the stranger: I am the Lord your God'(NKJV).

These last six words recur again and again in this chapter, like a recurring theme in a symphony. If we are God's people, our relationship with him should have a profound effect on all our other relationships. For he has given us his Spirit that our lives might be centres of compassion in a needy world. We *must* have unreaped edges in our lives for others.

Concern for others

There are the unreaped edges of *prayer*. When life gets busy, prayer can get squeezed out, and if we do pray we tend to reap the whole field of prayer for ourselves. And when life gets difficult we can get so preoccupied with our own problems that we forget about others. God certainly encourages us to pray for ourselves, and he gives us promise after promise to draw out believing prayer. But in all our prayer times, God wants us to leave room for others that *they* might benefit from our prayers.

Jesus made this very clear in his great Sermon on the Mount. He said, 'This … is how you should pray: "*Our* Father in heaven … Give *us* today *our* daily bread. Forgive *us our* debts, as we also have forgiven *our* debtors. And lead *us* not into temptation, but deliver *us* from the evil one"' (Matthew 6:9–13). So when we pray we should have God's family on our hearts, and name at least some of them in his presence. For they have the same sort of needs, and temptations, and problems that we have, and we can help them by our prayers. What a difference it makes in any church where the members really pray for one another. It affects the very atmosphere in which we meet for worship and fellowship. Resentments, quarrels and jealousies cannot survive in the place of prayerful concern.

In Luke 11, Jesus immediately follows the Family Prayer with a story about three friends. Having shown us *what* to pray for God's family, Jesus now shows us *how* to pray for them. We must be urgent and persevering, like the friend who stood between two other friends, one needing help, and the other giving help.

The first friend called unexpectedly, late at night. His travels had made him tired and hungry, but his friend had nothing to give him. His cupboards were empty. But he had another friend down the road who could provide what he needed, so he went to him. He wanted three loaves of bread, and he was determined not to leave without them. At first his friend was reluctant to help him, for he was tucked up in bed with his family, but his friend's shameless persistence brought him to the door to give him what he asked.

What a helpful picture of intercessory prayer! When we pray for others we stand between heaven and earth, to tap heaven's resources for earth's needs. Our own cupboards are bare, but we know where to get food. We can go to our Divine Friend who has everything, for our human friends who have nothing. And we must not be put off if he seems reluctant to help. We must never judge God by appearances or we shall misjudge him. The one big point that Jesus makes is, pray earnestly for your friends. Put your whole heart into those unreaped edges of prayer. God *will* answer you in his own way and time.

Love in action

Then there are the unreaped edges of *kindness*. Ephesians 5:18 commands us to 'be filled with the Spirit', and from that Paul launches a helpful passage on relationships. For when the Spirit controls us, our lives become oases of love in a selfish world. Galatians 5:22 says, 'The fruit of the Spirit is love', and what a difference that makes in our relationships, for it brings things like 'patience, kindness', and 'goodness' into our lives. We shall certainly keep unreaped edges for others.

In 1 John, the apostle brings our professed love to the bar of God's love, and he applies a very practical test. In 3:17 he says, 'If anyone has material possessions and sees his brother in need but has no pity on him, how can the love of God be in him?' How indeed, for the love of God gives, and acts, and serves. It is this kind of love that makes a church warm, welcoming, and attractive. There is a mutual concern for one another that spills over to any strangers that come in. No wonder John says in 3:18: 'Dear children, let us not love with words or tongue but with actions and in truth.' Loving feelings or loving words are not enough; we must put our love to work. We must have unreaped edges of generosity and kindness in our lives that will help and serve others.

A hurting world

There are also the unreaped edges of *sympathy*. We live in a world seamed with suffering. Trouble and trial abound. Natural disasters hit the headlines again and again. Earthquakes, typhoons, floods and famines wreck whole communities and can move us to tears. A newspaper headline on 19 January 2002 read: 'Thousands flee as fiery river of lava engulfs city'. The Nyiragongo volcano had erupted and destroyed the Congolese city of Goma. A UN official described is as 'a human catastrophe'.

And man's inhumanity to man constantly takes its toll. What evil was unleashed in New York and Washington on 11 September 2001! To think that men for their own selfish ends could fly two passenger planes into the twin towers of the World Trade Center, and another into the Pentagon in Washington, DC! It seemed unthinkable yet it happened, and our television screens portrayed the sheer horror of it all. And suicide bombers continue to make the headlines. But how destructive it all is! Such actions contribute nothing to the search for peace; they just perpetuate the circle of violence. I live in a province that suffered greatly from terrorism for some years so I have the seen the evil of it firsthand. Many families were callously and cruelly plunged into grief, and the legacy of pain remains.

Yes, we live in a hurting world. Sorrow, illness and disease have left a trail of shattered lives and broken hearts, like the track of a bleeding hare across the snow. In such a world we cannot live insulated lives. We *must* guard the unreaped edges of care and concern for they can mean so much.

In the local church, we cannot always visit those in need, but we could phone or write. And there are cards available today for all sorts of occasions. When my mother died, the letters and cards I received did not dry all my tears, but they did help, for they showed that others cared.

A church where there is genuine sympathy becomes a lovely haven of comfort for God's people. We can all play our part. For we can all ask the Lord Jesus with his own nail-pierced hand to etch the word 'Others' on our hearts. We mean business when we do that, for then we shall always have unreaped edges in our lives through which the Lord will enrich and encourage others.

When love breaks down

What tragic things can happen when love breaks down! Relationships fall apart, as many a family knows. And the same thing can happen in God's family. So the New Testament urges us to show 'brotherly love', for God wants his family cradled and nurtured in love. Romans 12:10 exhorts us to 'Be devoted to one another in brotherly love.' Hebrews 13:1 says, 'Keep on loving each other as brothers'. In 2 Peter 1, the apostle shows us the importance of adding to our faith, of pushing out its boundaries, and when he gets to relationships he says, 'add to your faith … brotherly kindness' (2 Peter 1:5–7).

But how unbrotherly we can be to one another! We find a vivid illustration of this in Nehemiah 5. This old story has some pertinent things to say to us about our relationships in the church. Unbrotherly conduct nearly wrecked God's work in Jerusalem, just as it can wreck God's work today. It can create havoc amongst God's people.

It divides our fellowship

For a start, *it divides our fellowship*. Nehemiah felt things deeply and in this chapter he gets very upset. His anger erupts like a volcano, and he showers the hearts of the guilty with his scorching words. He admits, 'I was very angry' (v. 6). The Jews were hit by famine, and like every other food shortage it brought rising prices. The people faced the scourge of inflation. They also groaned under the heavy weight of taxation. Their country lay under Persian control, and they had to pay taxes to the Persian king. And some people, as always, began to exploit the circumstances for their own gain. They had more ready cash than others, so they made loans at high rates of interest. They arranged mortgages under oppressive terms. Some of their clients, already mortgaged up to the hilt, could only get grain by selling their children into slavery.

How the rich moneylenders rubbed their hands at these arrangements! What an explosive situation! It made Nehemiah livid, and after pondering what he had heard, his anger against the nobles and officials boiled over. He accused them publicly of unbrotherly conduct. He said, 'You are selling your *brothers*' (v. 8), and the barbed rebuke in that word pierced their hearts and left them speechless. God's people are a family, but the whole concept of this had broken down. Brother was exploiting brother with a callous disregard of the consequences.

Care and concern

Family life only flourishes in an atmosphere of mutual care and concern. It must be rooted in love and respect. And in God's family we must do everything we can to foster a family spirit. In Jerusalem 'the men and their wives raised a great outcry against their Jewish brothers' (Nehemiah 5:1). They were suffering at the hands of their brothers, and that hurt. And the same thing can happen in the church.

It happened amongst the Christians at Corinth, as we learn from Paul's first letter to them. He rebukes them for their divisions and contentions. He refers to their envy and strife. They had split the church into factions, and quarrelling had broken out amongst them. Their treatment of one another was tearing the church apart.

Paul pleads with them to settle their quarrels and to live at peace. And in 1 Corinthians 1:10 he has two strong grounds of appeal. He says, 'I appeal to you, brothers, in the name of our Lord Jesus Christ, that all of you agree with one another so that there may be no divisions among you and that you may be perfectly united in mind and thought.' They belonged to Christ, they had a common allegiance to him, and so Paul pleads with them 'in the name of our Lord Jesus Christ'. That was his first ground of appeal. And because they belonged to Christ they also belonged to one another. They were joint members in the family of God, so Paul pleads with them as 'brothers'. That was his second ground of appeal. Their unbrotherly conduct was denying the very nature of the church, and destroying their family life.

When God saves us he adopts us into his family, and that binds us together in a unique fellowship. The church is our family, and we must keep that constantly in mind. What we do together we do as a family. When we worship together we come to exalt and magnify God, and to reach out to him as his children in faith and love. When we pray together we meet to transact family business. When we evangelize together we seek to bring others into God's family, that they too might know his forgiveness and peace. All these things are part of our family life.

How this should help us in our relationships! John Stott, the President of Christian Impact, in his exposition of 1 Corinthians 1, gives us some wise counsel. He says, 'Whenever we are conscious of tension with a fellow Christian, it is important that we should say to ourselves, "he is my brother", "she is my sister".' I have found that most helpful, for it puts God's perspective on things. It restrains us when we feel like hitting out or hitting back. It provides us with a breathing space. It curbs the unruly tongue, and checks the unkind retort.

The right attitude

And it gives us a right attitude to one another, for it reminds us of what we have in common. With all our differences we have the same Father, and we belong to the same family. The Jews made too much of their differences, so they knew more about division than fellowship. They had made differences of wealth and poverty, position and prestige into barriers, and that posed a serious threat to their life as God's people. They had a wrong attitude to one another. Nehemiah took them severely to task, for such differences should never become barriers in the family of God.

They may divide men and women in the world, but they should never divide men and women in the church. Paul makes this point very powerfully at the end of Galatians 3. He says, 'You are all sons of God through faith in Christ Jesus … There is neither Jew nor Greek, slave nor free, male nor female, for you are all one in Christ Jesus' (vv. 26, 28). Paul picks out three of the differences that in his day proved so divisive, differences of race, class, and sex. They illustrate the many differences in the world today that can so easily become sources of envy and jealousy, pride and prejudice, mistrust and misunderstanding. But in Christ they melt away like dew in the sunshine of God's love. They still exist, but they no longer matter. They are no longer barriers to unity and fellowship.

We have a bond in Christ that makes these outward differences pale into utter insignificance. We belong to God's family, and that gives us a multitude of brothers and sisters across the world. It helps so much to view other Christians in that way. It gives us the right attitude in all our relationships with them. It guards us against that unbrotherly conduct that can so sadly divide our fellowship.

It destroys our testimony

But more than that, *it destroys our testimony*. Nehemiah did not mince his words. He said to the greedy nobles and officials, 'What you are doing is not right. Shouldn't you walk in the fear of our God to avoid the reproach of our Gentile enemies?' (5:9). What was happening amongst the Israelites was shaming them before the Gentiles. And the world watches *us* with the same eagle eyes. It soon spots trouble amongst us, for it expects us to be different. At the same time, it seems almost glad when things happen to suggest that we are not!

Broken relationships have left a trail of sadness and heartache across the pages of history. And the world is still littered with them. Greed and self-interest, misunderstanding and mistrust, are still the curse of society. But God's family should be different, for have we not been born again? Do we not have the Holy Spirit living within us? Do we not have the love of Jesus in our hearts?

Our relationships in the church form a vital part of our testimony to the world. How clearly that comes out in John 17, as the Lord Jesus pours out his heart in prayer. He prayed that we might be one—no broken relationships—'that the world may believe that you have sent me' (v. 21). Martyn Lloyd-Jones, in his book *Sanctified through the Truth*, says,

If Christians are to evangelize the world, they themselves must be right, there must be no contradiction between the message and the life … All our elaborate efforts to get people to come to church are going to be useless if, when they come, they find the message contradicted within the church herself.

A strong motive

Nehemiah urged God's people in Jerusalem to put things right for the sake of their testimony, and he gave them a very strong motive—the fear of God. He said, 'Shouldn't you walk in the fear of our God to avoid the reproach of our Gentile enemies?' (Nehemiah 5:9).

We seem to have lost this 'fear' today. We make so much of God's love that we tend to forget the sterner side of his character. He is kind and good, but he is also holy and righteous. The fear of God takes in both sides of his character. It is not so much the fear of what he will do to us, as the fear of what we shall do to him. It is a fear born of love, a fear that we shall dishonour God, or grieve him, or offend him in some way.

Nehemiah had this 'fear' in his heart. He had a deep sense of the greatness of God, which comes out in his prayer life. In 1:5, he prays, 'O Lord, God of heaven, the great and awesome God'. And this fear comes out in his daily life. In 5:15–16, he reminds the people that the earlier governors had placed a heavy burden on them. 'But,' he says, 'out of reverence for God I did not act like that. Instead, I devoted myself to the work on this wall.' Nehemiah had God's interests at heart. He did not want to see him dishonoured, so he said to the nobles and officials, 'Shoudn't *you* walk in the fear of our God?' (5:9).

This 'fear' will make us aware of God in every situation. If it grips our hearts as it gripped Nehemiah's heart, it will prove a powerful weapon in our fight against sin. Proverbs 3:7 says, 'Do not be wise in your own eyes; fear the Lord and shun evil.' When temptation comes in all its attractiveness and we find it difficult to 'shun evil'; the fear of God will strengthen our resolve, and reinforce our resistance. Paul puts it positively in 2 Corinthians 7:1 when he writes about 'perfecting holiness out of reverence for God.'

And this 'fear' will prove a powerful incentive to love and respect God's other children. Paul makes this clear in Ephesians 5:21, where he transfers this fear to Christ. He says, 'Submit to one another out of reverence for Christ.' This cuts deeply into our self-life, for by nature we want to promote ourselves. Submission rules this out. We are not to throw our weight around, or exploit others for our own advantage. We are to serve others, not use them for our own ends. If God gives us authority amongst his people we must use it wisely and well.

The apostle says, 'Submit to one another', so he commands mutual submission. Leaders must lead, and those they lead must respect their leadership, but no leader must lord it over God's people. We must submit together to the rule of Christ, and seek in everything to please him. How it must sadden him to see his family at loggerheads! Again and again in his

Word he exhorts us to love one another. When love breaks down it grieves *him*. How this should constrain us, as far as lies in our power, to live in harmony and peace with all our fellow-believers.

A stirring example

Nehemiah had been appointed governor of Judah, and previous governors had thought nothing of profiting at the expense of the people. They preserved their own life-style regardless of the unjust conditions around them that brought poverty and slavery. And they were simply claiming their rights, so it would have been no surprize if Nehemiah had done the same thing.

But he chose a different path. He says, 'I never demanded the food allotted to the governor, because the demands were heavy on these people' (5:18). Nehemiah waived his rights because he had a deep concern for the welfare of God's people.

This spring of concern began to bubble up even before he got to Jerusalem. One of his brothers told him how badly things were going, and in 1:4, he says, 'When I heard these things, I sat down and wept ... and fasted and prayed before the God of heaven.' Nehemiah shaped his tears into prayers, and this concern for God's people never ceased to flow. It washed away the selfishness that had dirtied the lives of so many of the nobles and officials.

When he remonstrated with them for their unbrotherly conduct, they had nothing to say. They could not accuse him of sleaze, for his life lay before them like an open book. He spoke to them from the platform of godly example. That made his words like arrows that pierced their hearts, bringing shame and conviction.

This concern that bubbled up in the heart of Nehemiah flowed from the heart of God. Nehemiah had become the channel of it, and so can we. Let us open our hearts to it everyday, that God's concern for his people may flow through us. Then we too will be an example, enriching whatever church we belong to, and enhancing its testimony before the world. Yes, what a scourge unbrotherly conduct has proved to be! It has so many damaging effects amongst us.

It disrupts our work

For it not only divides our fellowship, and destroys our testimony, *it disrupts our work*. The trouble and unrest amongst God's people posed a serious threat to the rebuilding of the wall around Jerusalem. We can see the devil's hand in this. He is our great enemy, and he opposes God's work at every opportunity. He knows that dissension always brings disruption, so he sows the seeds of it wherever he can. He lurks in the shadows waiting to strike. He cannot make us sin, but he knows how to exploit our sinful nature. And he is a pastmaster at disguise. He works through others to accomplish his evil purposes; he seldom, if ever, comes out into the open.

He had already tried to stop God's work in Jerusalem. He had mounted attacks from outside the city, using the Jews' enemies, but his attacks failed. The people just went on building. But Satan does not give up easily. He launched another attack, this time from within. He turned his big guns on God's people themselves, concentrating his fire on their relationships. Anything to disrupt the work! And he still attacks in this way today. He encourages selfishness and vanity, pride and greed, and other wrong motives to stir up strife amongst us. He sets Christian against Christian, for when we are fighting amongst ourselves we get distracted from God's work Family rows do not help the family business, which is to get the gospel out.

Bickering Christians and divided churches bear tragic testimony to the devil's successes. Writing on this theme in his book, *Day by Day*, Vance Havner protests at 'the miserable divisions and tumults among believers today'. He says we have no right to accept them as normal, and how right he is. We should see Satan's hand in all this, and learn to resist him as Nehemiah did. He dealt with the situation head-on, with promptness, boldness, and thoroughness.

Be prompt

Nehemiah did not act hastily. He took time to think about the accusations that were being made, but then he took prompt and decisive action. He says, 'I pondered them in my mind and *then* accused the nobles and officials' (5:7). He challenged them without delay. Nehemiah's priority was that wall, and nothing must be allowed to stop the rebuilding of it. How vital that dissension in the church is dealt with promptly! If we leave it, it will fester like a sore. It will not go away, it will get worse. People will take sides and become hostile and divisive. So we dare not allow grudges or bitterness or animosity to drag on unfaced and unchecked. We must give them no hiding place in the basement of our hearts, and we must refuse to feed them. Broken relationships in the church grieve the Spirit and hinder revival. They disrupt God's work and distract God's workers.

Let us check *our* relationships and make sure that we are living at peace with all men, as far as lies in our power. If we are harbouring a grudge or a grievance, let us deal with it, for God's sake, for the work's sake, for others' sake, and for our own sake. Let us take any action that may be necessary.

Be bold

Nehemiah brought the whole thing out into the open. He spoke to the guilty nobles and officials first, and then he says, 'I called together a large meeting to deal with them' (5:7). It took courage to do that.

It *does* take courage to deal with broken relationships. The Lord Jesus made that clear in Matthew 18:15–17. He says, 'If your brother sins against you, go and show him his fault, just between the two of you. If he listens to you, you have won your brother over.' It is a family matter, and should be dealt with as one brother, or one sister, to another. 'But if he will not listen,' says Jesus, 'take one or two others along, so that "every matter may be established by the testimony of two or three witnesses." If he refuses to listen to them, tell it to the church', which means, bring it out into the open. Unbrotherly conduct should be dealt with in a brotherly way, as long as is it possible to do so. But if a personal effort at reconciliation breaks down, Jesus says, 'tell it to the church'. For these broken relationships involve the whole family. They affect our family life, as they affected the life of Israel.

In Matthew 5:23–24, Jesus also said, 'If you are offering your gift at the altar and there remember that your brother has something against you, leave your gift there in front of the altar. First go and be reconciled to your brother; then come and offer your gift.' The words, 'First go and ... then come', underscore the vital link between our relationship with God and our relationships with one another. Any breakdown in these relationships involves the Father as well as the family. How important it is then, that we live together in harmony and peace. In both these passages Jesus throws the ball into our court. Whether we have a grievance against our brother, or whether he has a grievance against us, Jesus tells us to take the initiative. We tend to dig our heels in, especially if we are harbouring a grievance, and we say, 'I'm not going to make the first move!' The Lord Jesus commands us to do just that. He makes *us* responsible for our relationships. It takes courage to try and put wrong things right, but if we deal with broken relationships the Lord's way, we can look to him for his help. If we all did that, there would be far less trouble in the church. It would be nipped in the bud before it could spread.

Be thorough

When trouble comes we tend to sweep it under the carpet. We tend to ignore it, and hope it will go away. Or we deal with it too superficially. But trouble amongst believers is like a weed; it has roots that go out of sight. To get rid of the weed we must get at the roots, or it will simply grow again.

Nehemiah dealt with the situation in Israel very thoroughly. He did not say to the people, 'You must pray about it', although prayer does help. It opens us up to God, and brings him into things. But such unbrotherly conduct demanded more than prayer.

Neither did Nehemiah say to the people, 'You must submit to the Lord in this. You must be more spiritual. You must accept this situation from him'. That would never have purged the resentment in the hearts of God's people. Sometimes we *have* to submit for we can do nothing to change things. But we should never submit to injustice if wrong things can be put right.

Nehemiah showed wise leadership. He dealt firmly with the offenders, and charged them explicitly with their offence. And he went to the root of the trouble, demanding immediate action. In 5:11–12 he says, 'Give back to them immediately their fields, vineyards, olive groves and houses, and also the usury you are charging them.' And the culprits confessed their sin saying, 'We will give it back.' And they repented, for they said, 'We will not demand anything more from them.' Then they made restitution, for they said to Nehemiah, 'We will do as you say.'

But Nehemiah left nothing to chance, for he knew their fickleness. He knew that greed stalked the corridors of their hearts, threatening to take control. So he made the nobles and officials take an oath, and they said that they would do what they had promised. And he shook out the folds of his robe and said, 'In this way may God shake out of his house and possessions every man who does not keep this promise. So may such a man be shaken out and emptied!' (v. 13). Nehemiah's promptness, boldness, and thoroughness paid dividends. For v. 13 says, 'At this the whole assembly said, "Amen," and praised the Lord. And the people did as they had promised.' Once again they could concentrate on God's work. Fences had been mended, relationships had been restored, and peace prevailed in Israel. The devil would attack again, but for the moment he fell back defeated. His attempt to drive disruptive wedges between God's people had failed.

If we all dealt with unbrotherly conduct before it got a hold in our lives, what a difference it would make to our relationships in the church. Many a difficult situation would be avoided, and God would be honoured, the gospel would be established, and the devil would be forced to concede defeat.

Me first

L ove has enemies that constantly threaten to destroy it, and we deal in this chapter with its greatest enemy, selfishness. The 'me first' syndrome runs right through our society, and it has a devastating effect on our relationships. It sparks countless arguments, quarrels, and conflicts. It lies behind all the social ills that blight the landscape of our nation. It plays a major part in the broken marriages and broken homes that cause so much grief and heartache. When self gets the upper hand it tramples all over those who impede its progress. It has left an ugly trail across the world that stretches right back to our first parents.

Ever since they turned their backs on God and embraced this 'me first' syndrome, the world has been in trouble. Genesis 1:27 says that, 'God created man in his own image', and that gave man the best possible start. But then he fell foul of the Tempter, who conned him into asserting his independence and insisting on his own way. In Genesis 5:3, we see one of the terrible effects of that: 'Adam … had a son … in his own image.' What a significant phrase! God's likeness in man had become sadly defaced, and it was that defaced image that Adam passed on. His son inherited his father's fallen nature, and the consequences of that reach right down to the present day.

Selfishness, with all its potential for disaster, lurks beneath the surface of every life. It can erupt at any time, like a volcano, and what damage it can do! It shows itself in different ways, some more objectionable than others. And some have more control over it than others, but it threatens all of us. And it can work havoc in our relationships. We see evidence of that all around us, as well as in our own lives.

Christian conflict

When God saves us we undergo a radical change. He gives us a new nature, and the centre of our life changes from self to Christ. That has a profound effect on the way we live; and it has a transforming effect on our relationships. But the old self does not give up the control of our lives without a struggle. It resents and resists the rule of Christ, who demands our total allegiance. He comes to us by his Spirit to set up his kingdom in our hearts. And he has no time for the 'me first' syndrome which devastates our lives, and that sets up the conflict that every Christian knows.

Paul describes it in Galatians 5:17: 'For the sinful nature desires what is contrary to the Spirit, and the Spirit what is contrary to the sinful nature. They are in conflict with each other, so that you do not do what you want.' Petersen very helpfully defines 'the sinful nature' as 'a root of sinful self-interest in us'. So in the light of this battle within, we cannot just coast along in the Christian life, or this old self will hold us back and drag us down.

The way of victory

We must side with the Holy Spirit and contend against it as Paul urges us in v.16. He says, 'Live by the Spirit, and you will not gratify the desires of the sinful nature', or as Petersen puts it, 'you won't feed the compulsions of selfishness'. Paul maps out the only way of victory: partnership with Christ by his Spirit.

We could picture this conflict as two kings, both of which demand our allegiance. We cannot give our allegiance to both; we must take sides. And the cross, with all that Christ did to save us, compels us to side with *him*. As Paul argues in 2 Corinthians 5:15, Christ 'died for all, that those who live should no longer live for themselves but for him who died for them and was raised again'. Christ won the battle of Calvary, and defeated all the forces arrayed against us, so that gives him the right to take full possession of our lives, and to penetrate and occupy our whole nature by his Spirit. But the sinful nature continues to dig in and resist him. The Lord still meets opposition, and still encounters pockets of resistance.

'Live by the Spirit', says Paul, charting the only way of victory. Live under the constant, moment-by-moment direction, control, and guidance of the Holy Spirit. For that to happen, we must force the old self to abdicate. In Matthew 16:24, Jesus says to his disciples, 'If anyone would come after me, he must deny himself and take up his cross and follow me.' We must give *him* the throne of our hearts, for he alone has the right to rule over us. We must yield unreservedly to him, and put ourselves at his disposal. And we must take our stand, day by day with him against all the yearnings of our sinful nature.

It will not be easy, for the old self is deeply entrenched, and sometimes we have to recover ground from him again and again. And like a spy in the castle he opens gates to the enemy. The battle will go on until our dying day, so we must be on our guard, and keep close to the Saviour.

The local church

Peace amongst God's people flourishes as we get the victory over the old nature. Paul demonstrates this in his Letter to the Philippians. He loved the Christians at Philippi and his concern for them shines out on every page. He kept them in his prayers for he had them in his heart, as he tells them in 1:7. And he wanted nothing to spoil their united stand for the gospel, so it grieved him to see cracks beginning to appear in the façade of their unity.

In 1:27, he says, 'Whatever happens, conduct yourselves in a manner worthy of the gospel of Christ. Then, whether I come and see you or only hear about you in my absence, I will know that you stand firm in one spirit, contending as one man for the faith of the gospel'. In 2:2, he says, 'make my joy complete by being like-minded, having the same love, being one in spirit and purpose.' In 4:2, he singles out two of the women in the church, and implores them to settle their differences. He says, 'I plead with Euodia and I plead with Syntyche to agree with each other in the Lord.' For when two people fall out, the ripples can spread right through the church, as others begin to take sides.

Self unmasked

In 2:3–4, Paul traces this threatened discord and division, like some dirty river, to its source: the old nature. He unmasks it in all its ugliness. He says, 'Do nothing out of selfish ambition or vain conceit, but in humility consider others better than yourselves. Each of you should look not only to your own interests, but also to the interests of others.' For if the 'me first' syndrome gets control it will soon shatter the unity of God's people. Once in the saddle it will ride rough shod through the whole fellowship.

Selfish ambition

Paul picks out two of the most common ways it reveals itself, even in the church. He begins with 'selfish ambition'. Other translations have 'rivalry', 'factional motives', and 'acting for private ends'. Back of all these translations there lays the idea of self-will, which warps our thinking. We push ourselves to the front, we insist that we are always right, and we think we have a perfect right to criticize others, although *they* must not criticize us! For we want to be in control.

Martyn Lloyd-Jones, in his comments on this chapter, translates it as 'the spirit of faction'. He describes it as 'a kind of party spirit, a group mentality, the tendency to think solely in terms of certain prejudices'. It makes us unreasonable for it gives us tunnel vision. We insist that our country, or our party, or our group is right, and we refuse to look any further. We are blinded by prejudice so we never face the question, 'Is my country, or my party, or my group right or wrong?' Such blindness always leads to misunderstanding, discord, and strife.

Vain conceit

But Paul picks out another way in which this 'me first' syndrome reveals itself, and this probes even deeper into our hearts. He calls it 'vain conceit'. He brings us face to face with the pride that is the ultimate source of all our troubles. When man in the beginning swept God from the throne of his heart, he climbed on to it himself. He thrust himself into the centre of the picture. He made his own will his supreme authority, and he began to live for what *he* wanted, and what *he* desired. What a catastrophe!

Man turned into himself and became his own god, and that spelled trouble from the start. The clash with others who had done the same thing became inevitable. All the sins that pollute our world and even the church, flow from the evil spring of pride. People demand their rights. They say, 'Why should I not live as *I* want?' And they think nothing of trampling on others to get their own way.

God hates pride for it strikes at the very foundations of his throne. Proverbs 16:5 says, 'The Lord detests all the proud of heart. Be sure of this: They will not go unpunished.' But we must not confuse pride with self-respect or a legitimate sense of personal dignity. The pride that God opposes is a haughty, undue self-esteem. It is what Billy Graham calls 'that repugnant egotism … that revolting conceit which swaggers before men and struts in the presence of the Almighty'.

Paul says, 'Do nothing out of selfish ambition or vain conceit' (Philippians 2:3), for these things can show their ugly faces even in the church, and when they do they destroy any semblance of unity. We must recognize them for what they are and resist them. But how do we do that?

Humility

With the word 'but' in 2:3, Paul turns a corner and points to a different path. He says, 'Do nothing out of selfish ambition or vain conceit, *but* in humility consider others better than yourselves.' Paul had followed this path himself so he is not saying, 'Go that way'; he is saying, 'Come this way'. And we can track his progress as his life unfolds.

He began as a go-getter with a burning ambition to get to the top. He belonged to the Pharisees who applauded themselves and despised others. They were noted for their self-conceit. Paul was determined to outshine his contemporaries, and he succeeded. He outstripped many of them in his zeal, which he poured into his ruthless persecution of the church. He even wanted to extend his murderous campaign to Damascus!

But then he met the risen Lord in that dramatic encounter on the Damascus Road. He had a vision of his glory that cast him to the ground. This once proud Pharisee lay in the dust, and from that moment his life began to change. He learned a new humility, for humility comes not from comparing ourselves with others, but comparing ourselves with the Lord Jesus Christ. It comes from looking at him. Paul grew up by thinking down.

In 1 Corinthians 15:9, he describes himself as 'the least of the apostles', and he has just a small group in mind. But some years later, in Ephesians 3:8, Paul takes a bigger step down, for he says, 'I am less than the least of all God's people', and he has the whole church in mind! Later still, in 1 Timothy 1:16, Paul takes an even bigger step down, for he describes himself as 'the worst of sinners', and he meant it. He had been reflecting on the enormity of his past sins, especially his violent persecution of the church, and it humbled him to the dust. Paul grew up by thinking down, and he urges us to do the same.

The example of christ

In Philippians 2:8 Paul says that Christ 'humbled himself', so *he* followed this path. And what giant steps down he took as he left his crown for a cross! We see in vv. 6–7 that he was 'in very nature God', but he was 'made in human likeness.' He cloaked his deity in humanity and came to an insignificant village, a humble cottage, a lowly mother, and a poor trade. He began his life on earth in a borrowed cradle; he ended it in a borrowed tomb; and during his ministry he had no home of his own. What luminous humility!

We get the punchline in 2:5, where Paul says, 'Your attitude should be the same as that of Christ Jesus.' What a searching word for all of us! Let us use it as a surgeon uses his knife to cut out all the false pride in our hearts.

'In humility', says Paul, 'consider others better than yourselves.' This will have a profound impact on our relationships, for as we go down in our own estimation others will go up. We must not push this to extremes, but even when we see a drunkard in the gutter we can say, 'There but for the grace of God go I.' Humility leaves no room for 'selfish ambition' or 'vain conceit'.

I find it helpful to trawl through Christian biography, and one day I netted a striking illustration of this in the life of Dr Alexander Whyte, who had such a fine ministry in Free St Georges in Edinburgh from 1870 to 1910. A friend called on him one day and told him that he had gone to hear an evangelist who was in town. He said, 'Dr Whyte, this man was lashing out at the ministers, and he said among other things that Dr Hood Wilson is not a converted man.' When he heard that, Alexander Whyte's face went dark with indignation. He leaped to his feet from his study chair and said, 'The rascal! Hood Wilson not a converted man! The rascal!'

His friend, startled by this display said, 'But that's not all, Dr Whyte. He said that *you* are not a converted man!' When he heard that, Dr Whyte stopped pacing up and down and just stood there. Then he walked over to his study chair and sat in absolute silence as he put his head in his hands. After a full minute he said, 'Please go, my friend, and leave me with my Lord to search my heart.' What humility!

Paul maps out the path that all God's people should follow when he says, 'Do nothing out of selfish ambition or vain conceit, but in humility consider others better than yourselves.' If we do walk this path we shall live in harmony and peace.

Extended horizons

In 2:4, Paul takes us further along this path. He says, 'Each of you should look not only to your own interests, but also to the interests of others.' With a skilful economy of words, Paul pushes our horizons back that we might see 'others' and not just ourselves. And the word he uses for 'look' is an unusual one. It means 'to fix one's attention on', like an archer aiming at a target. He has his eye on the bull, and he gives it all his attention and concern.

What a graphic picture of those who are so exclusively occupied with their own interests that they seem entirely oblivious of anyone else's. They are constantly aiming at the target of self-advantage, like Achan in Joshua 7. When he saw what the Israelites had plundered from the enemy his eyes lit up, for he sought his own enrichment, regardless of others. He wanted some of the gold, silver, and clothing for himself, so he took it with no thought of the effect it would have on his family. His story marks one of the Bible's accident black spots on the road of life. It says, 'Danger ahead! Take care!'

Paul, echoing this warning, puts this selfish outlook right out of court, for it has no place in the Christian life. The world encourages it. It says, 'Look out for Number One. If you don't, who will? Stand up for your rights!' And we must certainly look to our own interests, or life would fall apart, but we must look beyond them. We must not simply ask, 'What are my rights? What do I deserve? What's in it for me?' We must look at the other person and say, 'What's best for him?' or 'What's best for her?' This ties in with the second great commandment in Matthew 22:39 'Love your neighbour as yourself.' Instead of starting and ending with ourselves all the time we should look at others and their needs, their interests, their concerns. Life would be transformed if we all lived by this principle. So much of the trouble and unhappiness that sweeps over our world would be avoided.

Paul lets none of us off the hook, for he says, '*Each of you* should look not only to your own interests, but also to the interests of others' (Philippians 2:4). We must all work this out in our own lives, as Christ worked it out in his. Paul says, 'Your attitude should be the same as that of Christ Jesus' (2:5), and he goes on to demonstrate this attitude in a marvellous way in the verses that follow. What a sublime example of unselfishness! Christ came from heaven to earth with the word 'others' etched deeply on his heart, and his incredible concern for us took him to the Hill of Calvary to rescue us from the appalling consequences of our sin. He himself said, 'The Son of Man did not come to be served, but to serve, and to give his life as a ransom for many' (Matthew 20:28).

One day at the seaside I saw a line of footprints in the sand stretching out in front of me, and for a little way I followed them. And I thought of 1 Peter 2:21, which exhorts us to follow in Christ's steps, to walk as he walked, to live as he lived. But we cannot do that without his help, so let us seek that help each new day. Let us ask him that by his Spirit he will give us the resolve and the ability that we so much need.

A united front

In 2:2, Paul says, 'Make my joy complete by being like-minded, having the same love, being one in spirit and purpose.' He makes his plea very personal, and this strengthens the plea that he has already made in 1:27–28. He says, 'Whatever happens, conduct yourselves in a manner worthy of the gospel of Christ. Then, whether I come and see you or only hear about you in my absence, I will know that you stand firm in one spirit, contending as one man for the faith of the gospel without being frightened in any way by those who oppose you.'

Paul wanted them to close ranks and present a united front, for two very good reasons. First of all, they had a common Cause—'the faith of the gospel'. And, secondly, they had a common Enemy—'those who oppose you'. How can we pursue our own agenda with such big things at stake? They leave no room for 'selfish ambition' or 'vain conceit'. God has enlisted us in his army to plant the gospel standard in other lives and other lands, so we must stand shoulder-to-shoulder, especially in the face of Enemy resistance and Enemy attack.

I like the Hebrew of Zephaniah 3:9, which has the idea of serving the Lord 'shoulder to shoulder'. If you have ever seen a military march-past there is not a shoulder out of place; it looks just like one shoulder. What a great picture of a united front! If we have broken ranks in the church let us get back into line for the sake of the gospel.

Helpful influences

But pleas alone for humility, or unity, or unselfish living will not rid us of 'selfish ambition' or 'vain conceit'. We need more than that. We must expose ourselves constantly to the influences that Paul describes in 2:1–2. We must live daily in the atmosphere into which he brings us in these verses. He says, 'If you have any encouragement from being united to Christ, if any comfort from his love, if any fellowship with the Spirit, if any tenderness and compassion, then make my joy complete by being like-minded, having the same love, being one in spirit and purpose.' If we write the words 'as indeed you have' over vv. 1–2, it will take any uncertainty from Paul's repeated 'if'. He has no doubts about these things; he wants us to feel their full force.

The encouraging influence of Christ

Paul begins with *the encouraging influence of Christ*, for we cannot turn his teaching into practise without Christ. We need his help every step of the way. So Paul says, 'If you have any encouragement from being united to Christ'—and we have a wealth of encouragement. The Greek word that Paul uses, pictures someone standing with us to encourage us. Christ does that by his Spirit. He encourages us to pursue the path of peace. He encourages us to find solutions instead of taking sides. He encourages us to be patient with others as he is patient with us. He encourages humility and sacrifice and helpful relationships.

The closer we are to Christ the closer we shall be to one another, just as the spokes of a wheel are nearest at the centre. When we are conscious of him, rivalries, bigotries, intolerances and jealousies begin to lose their hold on us. Let us open our lives daily then, to the encouraging influence of Christ. Sin shatters relationships but Christ strengthens them.

The softening influence of love

Paul turns next to *the softening influence of love*. He says, 'if any comfort from his love', and the Greek word for 'comfort' means literally to speak closely to someone. It has an attractive intimacy about it. What a difference love makes in all our relationships. If only disgruntled Christians would luxuriate in the love of Christ, how it would soften their hearts towards others. Sin hardens but love softens. There can be no unity without love.

But how can we love those who are difficult to get on with? I heard of one man who had his own solution. He said, 'I've come to the conclusion that nobody really wants to be nasty and hateful and unpleasant, and if they are like that they must have a problem.' I find that helpful. It is not too hard to fight someone whom we think is being unpleasant, but we cannot feel good about making things more difficult for those grappling with problems.

Let us open our lives daily, then, to the softening influence of Christ's love. When it sweeps, flood-like, through our hearts, it will sweep away the ugly debris of selfishness, which can make us so hard.

The bonding influence of the Spirit

Then Paul turns to *the bonding influence of the Spirit*. He says, 'if any fellowship with the Spirit'. Bob Gillman gave us a most apt prayer when he wrote, 'Bind us together, Lord, bind us together with cords that cannot be broken, bind us together, Lord, bind us together, O bind us together with love.' For when God saves us he brings us into his Royal Family, he makes us his children, and we begin a new Family Life. We have brothers and sisters we never knew before, and the Holy Spirit wants to prosper our relationships, in and through Christ. He wants to bind us together, and he works to that end. So we can count on his help in our Christian fellowship as we seek to settle differences, and avoid quarrels, and live in peace.

And we need it so much! For the Spirit's ministry in our lives is crucial. The command comes echoing down the centuries, 'Be filled with the Spirit' (Ephesians 5:18). And how significant that that command leads into a long passage on relationships. Paul is saying, 'Let the Spirit have control. Let him do things with you, and you do things with him'. The Spirit-filled life means living in personal partnership with him. Let us open our lives continually then to the bonding influence of the Spirit. Sin divides but the Spirit unites.

The melting influence of compassion

Paul turns finally to *the melting influence of compassion*. He says, 'if any tenderness and compassion'. The Lord Jesus can make tough people tender, and that transforms relationships. We get a lovely example of that in Acts 16. When the Philippian jailor first met Paul and Silas he had no concern for them at all. A cruel beating had torn the flesh from their backs, but the jailor, insensitive to their sufferings, thrust them into an inner cell, and fastened their feet in the stocks. And he lost no sleep over them, for v. 27 tells us that he 'woke up'!

And when God used the earthquake that woke him to stab his conscience awake, he saw his need as never before, and he cried out, 'What must I do to be saved?' Through the ministry of Paul and Silas he came to faith in Christ, and the jailor knew a compassion he had never known before. God melted his heart, and one of the first things he did was to wash Paul and Silas's wounds.

The Lord Jesus can work miracles of change in peoples' lives. He can take even cannibals and make them Christians, and fill their hearts with love and tenderness. He did that amongst the Auca Indians, who martyred Jim Elliot and his companions when they tried to reach them with the gospel.

Let us open our lives more and more then, to the melting influence of compassion, for it will help us so much in our relationships. Sin toughens but love makes us tender.

Keep close to the Lord Jesus

The 'me first' syndrome cannot live amidst such influences. The encouraging influence of Christ, the softening influence of love, the bonding influence of the Spirit, and the melting influence of compassion leave the old self no room to do its divisive, destructive work. So let us keep close to the Lord Jesus, and open our hearts wide to these transforming influences. For then we shall walk the path of humility, unity, harmony and peace.

The menace of misunderstanding

B ut love faces other threats besides selfishness. As we pick our way through the minefield of relationships we must watch carefully for the mine of misunderstanding. It lies menacingly amongst us, just waiting to be triggered. Perhaps there is nothing more tragic and damaging amongst Christians than misunderstanding. It arises so easily, it spreads so swiftly, and the further it goes the worse it gets. The fall-out can be disastrous.

The Bible has a story about this that clothes it with flesh and blood. We find it in Joshua 22. It is a classic story of misunderstanding amongst God's people. We see how innocently it started, and how quickly it spread. And we see so clearly its potential for conflict. This old story speaks warningly to all of us, its lessons etched in history.

Israel had twelve tribes, and the two tribes of Reuben and Gad, and half the tribe of Manasseh, wanted to settle in Gilead on the east of Jordan. According to v. 9, God had given them what they wanted, but first they had to help the other tribes conquer and subdue the Promised Land. They did that, and after many victories, and with Joshua's gratitude and blessing, they returned to their chosen territory. Joshua was able to say to them, 'You have not deserted your brothers but have carried out the mission the Lord your God gave you' (v. 3).

When they reached the river, and before they crossed it, they built an imposing altar of witness to signify their national and religious oneness with the other tribes on the west of Jordan. They wanted to preserve their link with them. But the other tribes immediately and wrongly concluded that this was an idolatrous altar of sacrifice. They put the worst construction on it. They thought the two and a half tribes had become apostate. But it was all a misunderstanding!

Underlying reasons
If we examine the underlying reasons for this, we shall discover the

underlying reasons for most misunderstandings. They lie at the heart of the story, and they have been repeated again and again.

Hearsay

To begin with, *the action was judged too hastily*. Before they had time to weigh the evidence, the Israelites were spoiling for a fight. 'And when the Israelites heard that they had built the altar on the border of Canaan at Geliloth near the Jordan on the Israelite side, the whole assembly of Israel gathered at Shiloh to go to war against them' (vv. 11–12). What unseemly haste!

And it all began with hearsay: 'And when the Israelites *heard*.' Many a misunderstanding stems from hearsay. Some story is told, or some rumour is spread, and before any details are checked, judgement is passed. This happens all too often. A rumour can ripple through a church, and without checking the facts, too many members become judge and jury. If only more information was sought, many a misunderstanding would never arise.

Judging motives

Then *the motive was condemned too readily*. The building of this altar was certainly open to suspicion. The two and a half tribes were unwise to erect it without some word of explanation, for altars after all were used for sacrifice. We should do all we can to prevent other people misunderstanding our actions, but with the best will in the world we do not always succeed.

At the same time, why did the other tribes so readily condemn what the two and a half tribes had done? Why did they immediately brand the motive as evil and wrong? Why could there not have been some good intention behind it?

The deputation of eleven men that crossed from Israel gave the accused no opportunity to explain. They waded straight in with their accusations: 'How could you break faith with the God of Israel like this? How could you turn away from the Lord and build yourselves an altar in rebellion against him now?' (v. 16). The two and a half tribes were horrified that their action had been so misunderstood.

We should be very careful about judging other people's motives, for we cannot read their hearts. We do it too often. We see unkindness where it was not meant. We see slights where they were not intended. One woman said of another, 'I've been thinking she had thoughts about me which she never had!' Let us be more generous in our judgements. Let us give others the benefit of the doubt.

Jumping to conclusions

Then *the conclusion was drawn too quickly*. We all tend to do that. Instead of digging for facts we jump to conclusions. It is far less trouble! Hasty conclusions are almost always wrong conclusions. They certainly proved wrong on this occasion. And how disastrous they can be! If we kept our thoughts to ourselves the damage would be minimal, but if we have a juicy bit of gossip we want to pass it on! The news about this altar spread like a prairie fire! 'Have you heard?' 'Do you know?' 'Isn't it terrible!' How tongues wagged! Had the deputation not gone to Gilead, this hasty and wrong conclusion would have led to civil war.

But why do we jump to conclusions? Why do we listen to gossip that is damaging to others? Why do we put the ugliest construction on what others say and do? Why do we draw unfavourable inferences from mere rumours? Why do we so readily impute wrong motives to others? Maybe a fellow-Christian does slight us, or hurt us, or overlook us in some way, but why do we presume it was done deliberately? This repeated 'Why?' rebukes our hearts, and demands an answer.

The great accuser

Satan certainly plays his part in this. His name means 'accuser', and he is aptly named. He accuses men before God; he accuses God before men; and he accuses men before men. He is continually seeking to sow discord amongst God's people, and one of his most fruitful seeds is the seed of misunderstanding. It has been suggested that the area of the devil's quickest and deadliest activity is between someone else's remarks and my interpretation of them, between my fellow-worker's actions and my reaction. That should put us on our guard. But we cannot lay all the blame on Satan. Whatever else he can do, Satan cannot *make* us sin. 'A man can never say. 'I was overpowered in spite of myself', writes Griffith Thomas: 'All that he can say is, 'I was overpowered because of myself'.' Satan, or one of his aides can suggest evil thoughts about others, but he cannot *make* us entertain them. Why do we then?

A bias toward evil

Because by nature we have a bias toward evil rather than good, not only in what we do and say, but also in what we think. The Bible calls this inward bias the 'flesh' or 'the sinful nature'. When God saves us by his grace through faith in the Lord Jesus Christ, he does not remove this bias from our hearts. As we have seen already, it carries on its fifth column activities to the end of our days. It is like a spy in the castle that wants to throw it open to the ravages of the enemy.

God's way of victory is not eradication but counteraction. He gives us a new nature to counteract the old, and he gives us his Spirit to strengthen us for the conflict. Paul has a phrase in Romans 8:13 that I find most helpful: 'For if you live according to the sinful nature, you will die; but if *by the Spirit* you put to death the misdeeds of the body, you will live.' The Holy Spirit makes a powerful ally on the field of battle, when temptation begins to undermine our resistance. So to fight victoriously we must make Christ our Captain, we must yield daily to the Holy Spirit, and we must stand firm against sin.

Paul makes this very clear in Galatians 5. In vv. 16–17, he says, 'Live by the Spirit, and you will not gratify the desires of the sinful nature. For the sinful nature desires what is contrary to the Spirit, and the Spirit what is contrary to the sinful nature. They are in conflict with each other, so that you do not do what you want.' The Christian life has some lovely compensations, but it has this conflict in it that we cannot escape. We must keep close to the Lord Jesus if we are going to enjoy victory.

If we fail to live by the Spirit, the flesh will gain the ascendancy, and its power will prove too much for us. And one sphere of failure will be the sphere of personal relationships. If we are provoked we shall tend to think evil of others rather than good. For the beast of depravity still lurks within our hearts, and we need the constraints of Christ to keep it under control.

Living by the Spirit

If we live by the Spirit we shall know these constraints, for his love will fill our hearts and lives, and we shall have a magnanimous attitude to others. If we are provoked we shall tend to think good of others rather than evil, for love is not suspicious. It puts the best and not the worst construction on the words and actions of others, as long as it is possible to do so.

Tragic results

How eager we should be to know the victory of love, for this story illustrates the tragic results of misunderstanding. We see them in bud rather than in flower, for wiser counsels prevailed, but the results are here nevertheless. Misunderstanding can bring hurtful, harmful things in its train.

Hostility

It can bring *hostility*, as it did in Israel. And it can spread so quickly. It can tear God's people apart. In Joshua 22:12 we see the hostility of the nine and a half tribes gathering momentum until 'the whole assembly of Israel gathered at Shiloh to go to war against them.' Feelings ran high, for the people bitterly resented this provocative altar built by the other tribes. They streamed to Shiloh, their weapons in their hands, and they fully intended to use them.

What a tragedy, for the two and a half tribes had fought long and hard to help the other tribes bring the Promised Land under control. But now for all their efforts, their brothers had turned against them, and the threat of civil war hung in the air. And it all stemmed from a misunderstanding!

And the same thing can happen in the church. Misunderstanding can turn us against fellow-believers who have stood with us in God's work for many years. Some action is misjudged, some word is misconstrued, some omission is misinterpreted, and hostility, like some pernicious weed, can poison a teamwork God has greatly blessed. I have seen it happen. What a mercy that the hostile tribes used words before weapons! They sent Phinehas the priest and ten of the chief men across the Jordan to remonstrate with the other tribes. But they went spoiling for a fight. We can sense their hostility from what they said in vv. 16–20. They talked about treachery and purity of worship. They said, 'Your altar is an act of treason against God. It can only spell trouble!' And they went on to quote examples, and to speak of others like Achan who had sinned.

Had they not been so hostile they would have seen the wrongness of their approach. They should have sought an explanation before pronouncing their verdict. And we should do the same. But when relationships break down we think we are right and others are wrong. Many of us never question *our* understanding of the situation.

The Israelites thought *they* were right. Without seeking any explanation they thought they had the right interpretation of things. We can almost hear them say what one missionary remarked most 'sweetly' to his fellow-worker as they parted, 'Well, we've both tried to follow the Lord's will— you in your way, and I in his!'

The Israelites were happy enough about that altar when they discovered its true purpose; what made them angry was their interpretation of its purpose! What a lesson for all of us. Is there anything more tragic than a groundless hostility amongst God's people? Let us think good things about others as long as it is possible to do so. Let us give each other the benefit of the doubt.

Disunity

And misunderstanding can bring *disunity*, as it did in Israel. Until now all the tribes had been fighting together against a common enemy. They had stood shoulder to shoulder in battle after battle. They had a common purpose and a common aim. But this misunderstanding shattered their unity like a brick dropped on a sheet of glass. They looked out over the deep chasm of civil war. The nation's very existence hung in the balance, imperilling the whole future.

And how often misunderstanding brings disunity in the Christian Church. How it disrupts fellowship; how it spoils relationships; how it dishonours the name of the Lord Jesus; and how it grieves the Holy Spirit. Dr Graham Scroggie saw to the heart of things when he wrote, 'I venture to say that if all misunderstandings existing at present amongst Christians were cleared up, the Christian Church would be in a state of revival.'

The apostle Paul yearned for the unity of God's people, and his longing keeps surfacing in his letters. When he heard that cracks had begun to appear in his beloved fellowship at Philippi, as we saw in the last chapter, he wrote to the Christians there, urging them to fight the real enemy, and not to waste their ammunition on one another. He wanted them to stand 'firm in one spirit, contending as one man for the faith of the gospel' (Philippians 1:27). He wanted them to demonstrate their unity in Christ, and to put their problems behind them. In 2:2, Paul says, 'make my joy complete by being like-minded, having the same love, being one in spirit and purpose.' In 4:2, he addresses two of the members by name. He says, 'I plead with Euodia, and I plead with Syntyche to agree with each other in the Lord.' For united we stand but divided we fall.

Satan knows that, and works constantly to bring division. He knows how to exploit the differences that inevitably arise amongst us. He knows how to use misunderstanding to set God's people at loggerheads. Let us recognize his tactics, and be on our guard. Let us not jump to hasty conclusions. Let us put the best and not the worst construction on what others say and do, as long as it is possible to do so.

A happy resolution

What a disaster if the twelve tribes had gone to war! No doubt the hotheads encouraged it; you get them in every society. But while some wanted an army to deal with the situation, others planned a deputation. The men appointed went in a hostile mood but at least they went. And two things led to a happy resolution of this misunderstanding.

Explanation

At last the two and a half tribes got an opportunity *to explain what they had done*. But we have to read down to Joshua 22:21 before we read their reply. Phinehas and the others insisted on having their say first, and they spoke at length. They wanted to nip this 'rebellion' in the bud before it got any worse. But if they had sought an explanation first, before jumping to conclusions, this ugly situation would never have arisen.

The leaders of the tribes in Gilead said, 'We had no intention of rebelling against the Lord. We built that altar because we were scared for our children. We had no symbol, no reminder, and with the Jordan between us, we saw the danger of being cut off from you. Please don't think that we were trying to become independent; we wanted to keep our links with you. And we did not build that altar to turn away from the Lord and to offer burnt offerings and grain offerings, or to sacrifice fellowship offerings on it. We meant it to be an altar of witness that we have a share in the Lord just as you have.'

They wanted their descendants to be able to say, 'Look at the replica of the Lord's altar, which our fathers built, not for burnt offerings and sacrifices, but as a witness between us and you' (v. 28). As the situation was set and seen in a different light one can almost hear an audible sigh of relief. The two and half tribes' explanation cleared the air, and the deputation's icy hostility melted away in the warm sunshine of understanding. The word 'pleased' in v. 30 spotlights the dramatic change that took place in Phinehas and his colleagues. If only they had sought an explanation first instead of going to Gilead with such bitter accusations!

Let us learn from their mistake. Let us be slow to judge, for many a misunderstanding amongst Christian people would be avoided if an explanation were sought before any judgement was passed. If only we could be more open with one another! There is nearly always an explanation if we are humble enough to seek it.

Acceptance

The deputation from Israel *accepted* the explanation that the leaders in Gilead gave them, and rejoiced in it. This is so important. They did not hang on to their suspicions. They did not say, 'We don't believe you.' They were glad to have the matter cleared up.

When we are seeking to clear up a misunderstanding, we too must be willing to accept the explanation that is given. We must listen sympathetically, not suspiciously. We must credit other Christians with as eager a desire to follow the Lord as we have ourselves. We must be willing to admit that we are partly if not wholly to blame for the misunderstanding, humbling though that is.

Misunderstanding flourishes in the suspicious, over-sensitive mind; it flourishes in those who are always on the defensive and go round expecting to be hurt. So let us ask the Lord Jesus for that generous spirit, that big heart, that loving nature that he alone can give us by his Spirit. Then if something goes wrong we shall approach it in the right way, and we shall be a part of the solution instead of being a part of the problem.

Specks and planks

Love faces another threat from a censorious spirit, which sours the atmosphere in any family. It makes harmonious relationships impossible, for it undermines the love and respect that bind a family together. If just one member keeps criticizing it spoils family life, for it can be so discouraging. And it has the same effect in the family of the church. The Lord Jesus sets up a warning light against it in Matthew 7, which is part of his Sermon on the Mount. And he is very clearly speaking to God's family in this Sermon for he uses the words 'father' and 'brother' again and again.

In v. 1, Jesus says, 'Do not judge, or you too will be judged.' What a sobering thought! By judging others we bring judgement on ourselves. For we are claiming to know what should or should not be done. And both God and men will use the standards we impose on others, to judge us. 'For in the same way as you judge others,' said Jesus, 'you will be judged, and with the measure you use, it will be measured to you' (v. 2). That should check those hasty, unkind criticisms that spring all too readily to our lips!

Self-criticism

But Jesus probes deeper. He insists on self-criticism. He says that before we criticize others we should take an honest look at ourselves, and he drives this point home with a startling picture. In vv. 3–4, he says, 'Why do you look at the speck of sawdust in your brother's eye and pay no attention to the plank in your own eye? How can you say to your brother, "Let me take the speck out of your eye," when all the time there is a plank in your own eye?'

Specks and planks! What a ridiculous contrast, but see how effectively Jesus uses it to make his point. Charles Spurgeon used to say, 'You must tickle the oyster to get the knife in', and Jesus certainly gets the knife in here. With humorous hyperbole he exposes the hypocrisy of criticizing others for the very things we tolerate in ourselves, only greatly magnified—from a speck to a plank.

We can be so inconsistent, and so blind to our own faults. In a Connecticut city, in America, fifty-three residents of a certain neighbourhood signed a petition to stop reckless driving on their streets. The police set a watch. A few nights later they caught five people, and all five had signed the petition!

Jesus' words in v. 5 penetrate our hearts like a rapier. He says, 'You hypocrite, first take the plank out of your own eye, and then you will see clearly to remove the speck from your brother's eye.' So before we look at others we should take a long hard look in the mirror. That will leave no room for the critical spirit that the Lord Jesus condemns in these verses.

Helpful criticism

But Jesus does not outlaw criticism altogether, for he says, 'first ... your own eye, and then ... your brother's eye.' He says, 'first ... the plank ... and then ... the speck'. So criticism, like removing a speck of sawdust from our brother's eye, can be most helpful. It all depends on our motive, our approach, and our attitude. As Abraham Lincoln put it, 'He has a right to criticize who has a heart to help.'

It is by criticism that we improve. It is by criticism that hidden faults are exposed. It is by criticism that we uncover things that are wrong so that they can be put right. And it is by criticism that we guard the truth, and escape from error.

We must use our critical faculty for we live in a world full of lies, and other people are not always what they seem to be. In v. 6, Jesus says, 'Do not give dogs what is sacred; do not throw your pearls to pigs.' By 'dogs' and 'pigs' he meant unholy people who would not appreciate holy things. In v. 15, he says, 'Watch out for false prophets.' So we cannot be uncritical or we shall be deceived very easily. We must employ sensible criticism that discerns and evaluates.

The dangers

But criticism is not an easy thing to handle. If used wisely it can be most helpful, but if used wrongly it can be most harmful. We must steer a course between gullibility on the one hand and censoriousness on the other. Criticism has hidden dangers lurking in it, and Paul uncovers them in Romans 14. A critical spirit had crept into the church at Rome, as it creeps into so many churches, and the apostle wanted to put a stop to it before it did any more damage. So in v. 13, he says, 'Let us stop passing judgement on one another,' and he shows us how criticism can get out of hand.

Pride

Censoriousness has some very nasty roots, and Paul exposes them in this chapter. He deals first with *pride*. In v. 4, Paul says, 'Who are you to judge someone else's servant? To his own master he stands or falls.' The apostle drags out the pride that hides within a critical spirit. He says, 'Who do you think you are, criticizing another man's servant? You take too much on yourself.' What an evil thing pride is, and how it persists even in the hearts of God's people. Ridding ourselves of pride has been likened to peeling an onion. When we take one skin off we find another skin underneath. Only the Lord Jesus can rid us of pride, and he can rid us of every layer of it. But if pride still holds sway in our hearts we shall be quick to judge, for pride thrusts self into the centre of the picture. It makes self the standard by which we criticize others. Paul pricks this balloon of self-importance when he says, 'Who are *you* to judge someone else's servant?' But what kind of pride lurks behind a critical spirit?

Our supposed righteousness

It could be pride in the supposed righteousness of our own lives. We may not claim to be better than others, but that is what our criticisms often imply. Self-righteousness always makes us critical of others. We see that in the Pharisees. One day Jesus told a parable against them because they 'were confident of their own righteousness and looked down on everybody else' (Luke 18:9).

He described two men praying in the Temple, a Pharisee and a Tax Collector. The Pharisee cut a very fine figure and doubtless had many admirers, but his prayer exposes a heart steeped in self-righteousness. He was so pleased with himself. He says, 'God, I thank you that I am not like other men—robbers, evildoers, adulterers—or even like this tax collector' (v. 11). And he looked down his nose at the other man who stood praying beside him. Then he took out his own religious CV that he had written in the most glowing terms, and gave that to God. He only quoted an extract from it, but he thought that was enough. He said, 'I fast twice a week and give a tenth of all I get' (v. 12).

How different from the tax collector who hung his head and beat his breast and said, 'God, have mercy on me, a sinner' (v. 13). He had no religious CV to give to God. He did not have a good word to say for himself, but God accepted *him* as righteous, not the Pharisee. Jesus said, 'I tell you that this man, rather than the other, went home justified before God. For everyone who exalts himself will be humbled, and he who humbles himself will be exalted' (v. 14).

The Pharisee prided himself on his own righteousness, but the Bible tears down any such self-built facade no matter how good it looks. Romans 3:10 says, 'There is no-one righteous, not even one'. That should purge the pride from our hearts, for the words 'no-one' and 'not even one' indict every one of us. They allow no exception. Judged by God's standards we *all* need his mercy, so what right have we to sit in judgement on others?

Recently, a prominent minister left his wife for another man, and it made headline news. It sent shock waves through the ranks of God's people. In the light of his Word such conduct is wrong and can never be condoned. It dishonours God, and brings the gospel into disrepute. But how careful we must be not to lapse into self-righteousness, and point the finger condemningly as though we were free from temptation. 1 Corinthians 10:12 warns all of us, 'If you think you are standing firm, be careful that you don't fall!' The nasty weed of censoriousness will never grow in the lovely soil of humility.

Our own views

But the pride entrenched in a critical spirit could also be pride in the supposed rightness of our own views. It was this that had opened the floodgates of criticism amongst the Christians in Rome, for they had different views about things. Some were vegetarians and others were not. Some were observing special days and others were not. Both groups thought they were right, and they could give their reasons, but it did not stop at that. They started sniping at those who disagreed with them. Paul exposes and condemns this critical spirit, and he goes to the core of it by asking, 'Who are you to judge someone else's servant? To his own master he stands or falls' (v. 4).

We must distinguish, of course, between essentials and non-essentials.

We must defend God's revealed truth at all costs, but even then we m[...]
it humbly. When it comes to the non-essentials and those matters on which
we have no clear guidance, if we cannot agree, we must agree to differ.
There must be mutual toleration. If we insist that everybody must agree
with us, and criticize those who do not, even questioning their spirituality,
we fall foul of arrogant pride. Let us ask the Lord Jesus to root from our
hearts every vestige of this poisonous weed.

Dr Paul Rees, the American preacher, quotes a friend of his who once
said to him, with a twinkle in his eye, 'In my life-time I've had little trouble
with people's convictions, but a lot of trouble with their opinions.' Let us
be firm in our convictions, but flexible in our opinions, and humble at all
times.

Prejudice

We can use criticism in two ways. We can use it to help others, or we can use
it to hurt others. We can use it as a tool to build others up, or we can use it as
a weapon to bring others down. We *do* use it as a tool but, sadly, we also use
it as a weapon. For another root of censoriousness is *prejudice*. Criticism is
often a symptom of something else, so our judgement is impaired from the
start. We criticize without sifting the facts because our minds are made up
already. In Romans 14, Paul seeks to put every kind of prejudice right out of
court.

Dislike

Sometimes prejudice is due to dislike. If we dislike someone, criticism
makes a handy weapon to use against them. We may make criticisms of our
own, or we may pass on the criticisms of others. We may even look for
things to criticize!

When I received a call to one of the churches I served, a couple opposed
to the call visited two of my previous churches on a fault-finding mission.
They tried, in vain, to find some dirt they could throw at me. They did not
know me personally. They were driven by dislike rooted in prejudice.

The only way to deal with this kind of criticism is to bring it into the
presence of the Lord Jesus and look at it honestly. We must recognize and
confess the dislike that triggers it off. We may begin by disliking what other

people do—that was happening in the church at Rome—then transfer that dislike to the people themselves. Only the Saviour can rid us of this. He can give us a love in our hearts that will kill the criticism on our lips. Spiteful criticism cannot live in the atmosphere of love.

Jealousy

But sometimes the prejudice that lies behind censoriousness is due to jealousy, and what a horrid thing that can be. When we fall foul of jealousy, the tongue becomes a ready instrument of nasty, spiteful, destructive criticism.

It is becoming clear that censoriousness often masks something else, something even worse. Dr Sangster, in his little book, *He is Able,* has a chapter entitled, 'When Jealousy Invades My Heart'. In that chapter he writes, 'Let us suspect ourselves when we begin to sneer at other people's success, when we imply that the businessman's progress was probably the result of sharp practice; or the public speaker's gifts rather flashy and superficial things with no solid merit beneath them; or the beautiful girl, who has excited our envy, not so beautiful in character and disposition as her face would imply.'

Jealousy has been defined as 'envy born of some deep love of self', and only the Lord Jesus can deliver us from it. He alone can uproot it from our hearts and plant the lovely flower of magnanimity in its place.

Resentment

And sometimes the prejudice behind this wrong kind of criticism is due to resentment. Perhaps somebody offends us, or wrongs us in some way, and we begin to harbour a grudge. We want to hit back and when that happens, spiteful criticism becomes a handy ready-made weapon. If there is somebody we almost enjoy criticizing, we should suspect ourselves immediately. Something has crept into our hearts that should not be there.

Again, only the Lord Jesus can give us the inner victory we need. So let us surrender our resentment to him, or if that proves difficult let us ask him to help us surrender it. He can fill us with his love so that every trace of resentment melts away.

Impaired judgement

Prejudice, whatever its cause, poisons our feelings and impairs our judgement. It blinds us to our own faults and sharpens us to detect the faults of others. We see the darkness in others but not in ourselves. We must learn to use the mirror of self-examination, for this judging of others is fraught with danger, as Paul points out in Romans 14:12. He says, 'Each of us will give an account of *himself* to God.' That should make us very hesitant about criticizing others. Paul follows with a strong 'Therefore'. In v. 13 he says, 'Therefore let us stop passing judgement on one another.'

We may try and justify our carping criticisms by saying we only want to help. Paul seems to anticipate that, for he tells us how to be really helpful. He says, 'make up your mind not to put any stumbling-block or obstacle in your brother's way' (v. 13). That should make us look at ourselves before we try and put others right.

Presumption

Paul throws out some probing questions in this chapter, designed to make us think. In v. 4, he says, 'Who are you to judge someone else's servant?' In v. 10, he says, 'You, then, why do you judge your brother? Or why do you look down on your brother?' We can be far too free with our criticisms and not realize what we are doing. But what *presumption*!

The apostle describes us as servants and brothers. We are servants working for the same Master, so what right have we to judge one another? The Master himself will judge us. We are also brothers and sisters in the same family, so how sad that we should judge one another. How it grieves our Heavenly Father! And we do criticize one another, far too often, and we are all guilty. Paul underscores this in Romans 14, and shows us how serious it is.

Usurping the position of Christ

For one thing we usurp the position of Christ. If we are Christians, Christ is our Master and we are fellow servants, so when we judge one another we take too much on ourselves. Paul punches this home in v.4 by asking, 'Who are *you* to judge someone else's servant? To his own master he stands or falls.' So when we sit in judgement on our fellow-believers we are behaving like masters not servants, and implying that they are responsible to *us* for what they do. What presumption!

Paul writes this chapter against the backcloth of Christ's Lordship. 'Whether we live or die,' says Paul, 'we belong to the Lord. For this very reason, Christ died and returned to life so that he might be the Lord of both the dead and the living' (vv. 8–9). He holds a unique position amongst us, and we are all responsible to *him* for the way we live. Let us remember this the next time we are tempted to sit in judgement on one another. We have no right do that, for we are usurping the position of Christ.

Anticipating the judgement of Christ

How trenchantly Paul argues against censoriousness in vv. 10–13! He begins with a disturbing 'Why?' He says, 'You, then, why do you judge your brother? Or why do you look down on your brother?' Why indeed? We have no right to sit on Christ's judgement throne for we shall be amongst the judged. 'For we will all stand before God's judgement seat. It is written: "As surely as I live," says the Lord, "Every knee will bow before me; every tongue will confess to God." So then, each of us will give an account of himself to God.' I like Eugene Petersen's paraphrase: 'You've got your hands full just taking care of your own life before God.' How true! 'Therefore', says Paul, 'let us stop passing judgement on one another.'

What a powerful argument against a critical spirit! The censorious Christian anticipates the judgement of Christ but forgets that he must face that judgement himself. Again, what presumption! Paul with his unique apostolic authority says, 'We will *all* stand before God's judgement seat'. That should cure of us of this wrong kind of criticism if nothing else does! Judgement is coming even for God's people. On that day Christ himself will judge us, individually, and fix our eternal rewards. We have no right to anticipate that day.

In 1 Corinthians 4:5, Paul says bluntly, 'Judge nothing before the appointed time.' How that indicts the censorious Christian! Paul says, 'Wait till the Lord comes. He will bring to light what is hidden in darkness and will expose the motives of men's hearts. At that time each will receive his praise from God.'

We are not qualified to judge

Christ's judgement will be all that our judgements are so often not. It will be positive—mark the phrase 'praise from God'. Our judgements are so often negative; we castigate, we blame, we find fault. And how often we criticize one another without knowing all the facts. We are not qualified to judge, for we lack the big picture. We cannot see into people's hearts. We cannot read their motives. We find it impossible to be totally objective. How often we have jumped to conclusions, and made judgemental statements, only to be proved wrong! How often we have had to modify our criticisms of others on closer acquaintance with them!

One day, a man was sitting in a railway compartment with a little baby on his knee. Not long after the journey started the baby began to cry, and try as he might the man could not pacify it. A passenger turned to the woman sitting next to him and said, 'Fancy him bringing a baby like that on this journey. I can't think why the mother would allow such a thing.' Lifting his voice a little he continued, 'I wonder where the mother is anyway? Perhaps she's gone off and left them!' The baby's father, overhearing what had been said, turned sadly to his critic and replied, 'I'll tell you where the mother is. She's in a coffin in the guard's van. She died two days ago, and I'm taking her back to the little village in which we were married, so that she can be laid to rest.' His words were met with an embarrassed silence. How careful we should be in the judgements we make!

If we resolved to criticize our criticisms before we made them, many of them would not reach our lips. There is a place for wise and sensitive church discipline, but that is a matter for the church, not the individual. What the Bible condemns is the personal censoriousness of the individual Christian. Both the Lord Jesus and his apostle put up warning lights against it for it endangers all of us. A preoccupation with the faults of others, blinds us to our own faults. It leaves us unprepared for *God's* day of judgement, when we shall *all* face the judgement that really matters.

Jesus' words about the speck and the plank help to drive home Paul's conclusion in Romans 14:13: 'Therefore let us stop passing judgement on one another. Instead, make up your mind not to put any stumbling-block or obstacle in your brother's way.'

Handling disagreements

Nothing triggers a censorious spirit amongst God's people more quickly than disagreements about the 'grey areas' of Christian conduct. They certainly test our Christian love! If we are not careful they can put us at loggerheads with one another and devastate relationships in the church. They are fraught with danger as the Christians in Rome discovered.

We know that some things are right because the Bible clearly commands them; and we know that other things are wrong because the Bible clearly condemns them. God maps out pathways of obedience in the Ten Commandments that every Christian should follow. He puts 'No Entry' signs on things like stealing, murder, and adultery, which leave no room for discussion. They are not subjects for debate. In Romans 13:12, Paul calls them 'deeds of darkness' and exhorts us to get rid of them as we would strip off dirty clothes. They have no place in the Christian life, and we would all agree with that.

But there are other things that the Bible neither commands nor condemns, so we must make up our own minds about them. As Paul puts it in Romans 14:5: 'Each one should be fully convinced in his own mind.' We must follow what Petersen calls, 'the convictions of conscience'. Paul himself did that, for in v. 14 he says, 'As one who is in the Lord Jesus, I am fully convinced that no food is unclean in itself.' That should settle the matter, but sadly it does not. These 'grey areas' often spell trouble, for Christians not only disagree about them, they want to legislate for others. They want to impose *their* list of dos and don'ts on other believers.

The Christians in Rome had differences of opinion about special diets. Some had no scruples about eating meat, but others were vegetarians. They had been saved out of paganism with its worship of idols and that coloured their thinking. They refused to buy meat sold at their local meat market because it was most likely part of an animal that had been offered in pagan worship. They thought that this tainted it so their consciences forbade them to eat it. Other Christians, who poured scorn on idols, did not believe that lifeless bits of wood or stone could in any way contaminate such meat whether it was part of an animal offered in worship at an idol shrine or... So they ate it without any qualms.

The Christians in Rome also had differences of opinion about special days. Some of them had been saved out of a Jewish legalistic background, and that coloured *their* thinking. They kept the Jewish holy days with clockwork regularity, for they considered them to be more sacred than other days. Their conscience would not permit them to do otherwise. Other Christians, with no such background, did not believe that one day was more sacred than another. They considered every day alike.

If we simply debated special diets and special days we would not tread on anybody's toes, for these things are no longer burning issues. Times have changed, dramatically. We have a different list of dos and don'ts today, but it can be just as divisive. For not every Christian compiles this list in the same way. There are many 'doubtful' things about which Christians have a difference of opinion.

We must tread carefully, for we enter a minefield of evangelical taboos. And we must bear in mind that they differ from one age to another, from one country to another, and from one culture to another, so we cannot draw up a complete list. Some Christians would never go to the cinema, or the theatre, or go dancing, or go to a football match, or play cards, or use make-up, or use alcohol, or smoke. They regard these things as worldly and insist that they are wrong for every believer. They treat them like fences at the top of a cliff, and they erect them to stop Christians toppling over into worldliness. We cannot fault their motive, for worldliness threatens all God's people, but not all Christians define it in the same way. They do not have the same list of taboos, and this can put them on a collision course with those who disagree with them.

Charles Swindoll, in his helpful book *The Grace Awakening*, has a chapter in which he exposes the ugly side of legalism. He tells the extraordinary story of a missionary family that liked peanut butter. But in the place where they were sent to serve the Lord it was not available, so they arranged with some of their friends in the United States to send them peanut butter every now and again, so they could enjoy it with their meals. But they ran into a problem. They discovered that the other missionaries considered it a mark of spirituality that you do *not* have peanut butter with your meals!

But the young family did not buy into that line of thinking; they kept getting regular shipments of peanut butter. They did not flaunt it; they just enjoyed it in the privacy of their own home. Charles Swindoll says, 'Pressure began to intensify. You would expect adult missionaries to be big enough to let others eat what they pleased, right? Wrong. The legalism was so petty, the pressure got so intense, and the exclusive treatment became so unfair, it finished them off spiritually … They finally had enough. Unable to continue against the mounting pressure, they packed it in and were soon homeward bound, disillusioned and probably a bit cynical.' What a tragedy! 'What we have here,' says Swindoll, 'is a classic modern-day example of a group of squint-eyed legalists spying out and attacking another's liberty. Not even missionaries are exempted.'

The weak and the strong

Paul identifies the two opposing groups in the church at Rome as the 'weak' and the 'strong', and he addresses both groups. And we get a surprise, for the 'weak' Christians are those who have a conscience about diets and days. They have not understood their liberty in Christ, or matured sufficiently in their faith to enjoy this liberty. In Romans 14:1–2, Paul describes them as weak in faith, not in saving faith, but in the application of their faith. And in 15:1, he refers to 'the failings of the weak'.

'Strong' Christians, on the other hand, refuse to accept the bondage of man-made rules. They will have their list of dos and don'ts, but they will draw it up for themselves, in fellowship with the Lord Jesus, and treat it as a guide not a chain. And they will certainly not insist that every other believer must live by it. They prize their liberty in Christ too much, and they want other Christians to enjoy it too.

Right attitudes

The real problem in the church at Rome was not diets and days but the Christians' wrong attitudes to one another, and they lie at the heart of *our* disagreements. In Romans 14–15, Paul uncovers the rejection, arrogance, pride, and contempt that were destroying Christian fellowship. And undergirding them all was a sad lack of love. No wonder the Christians at Rome found it hard to handle their disagreements! Paul seeks to correct these wrong attitudes by laying down certain principles that we should all take to heart.

Openness

First of all, we must open up to other believers, as flowers open up to the sun, for we all live in the sunshine of God's love. We all belong to the same family. God is our Father, and we are his children, and we must not close our hearts against his other children because their lists of dos and don'ts do not correspond with ours. We should never restrict our love by hedging it around with conditions like that.

Beneath the problem of diets and days in the church at Rome, and lurking out of sight like some dirty underground spring, lay a deeper problem, the problem of acceptance. So Paul starts with that, and brings it to the surface. In 14:1, he addresses the 'strong' in faith. He says, 'Accept him whose faith is weak, without passing judgement on disputable matters.' I like the vigorous pictures that Petersen uses in his paraphrase of these verses. He says, 'Welcome with open arms fellow believers who don't see things the way you do. And don't jump all over them every time they do or say something you don't agree with.'

Acceptance means treating other believers as brothers and sisters, without insisting that they dot all our 'i's and cross all our 't's. Christian fellowship should never depend on agreement about the 'grey areas' of Christian conduct. Charles Swindoll says, 'Let me give it to you straight. Don't give me your personal list of dos and don'ts to live by! And you can count on this: I will never give you my personal list of "do"s and "don't"s to follow. Being free means you have no reason whatsoever to agree with my personal list; nor should you slander me because it isn't exactly like yours.'

After all, if God has saved us *he* has accepted us, v. 3. What better reason could we have for accepting one another without hedging our acceptance about with our own rules and regulations? In 15:7, Paul says, 'Accept one another, then, just as Christ accepted you, in order to bring praise to God.' And Christ accepted *us* with open arms!

Humility

Secondly, we must get off our self-built and self-appointed pedestals. In

Chapter 7

Romans 14:2 Paul describes the situation in the church at Rome. He says, 'One man's faith allows him to eat everything, but another man, whose faith is weak, eats only vegetables.' As we look through the window of that verse we see differences of opinion, for God's people viewed things differently, and had they left it there, all would have been well. But they did not leave it there, as v. 3 makes clear. Paul says, 'The man who eats everything must not look down on him who does not, and the man who does not eat everything must not condemn the man who does, for God has accepted him.' The 'strong' were looking down on the 'weak', and the 'weak' were condemning the 'strong'.

But we cannot 'look down' on others, or 'condemn' others, without implying that *we* are more spiritual, that *we* stand on higher ground. What arrogance! Such a practice smacks of pride, for who gave us the right to pontificate on the 'grey areas' of Christian conduct? We must resist the temptation to 'play God' and allow others to make up their own minds. Paul says bluntly, 'Who are you to judge someone else's servant?' (v. 4).

God can make us stand
Sometimes we want to legislate for other Christians because we fear for them. Maybe they are new converts, and we want to throw a hedge around them. We think our list of dos and don'ts will protect them from the temptations of an ungodly world, but we take too much on ourselves. For God has not appointed *us* to be their conscience. They are not accountable to *us* for what they do. If God has saved them, then *he* is at work in their lives, and *he* can direct them. We must leave them with him. Paul makes this very point in v. 4. He says, 'Who are you to judge someone else's servant? To his own master he stands or falls. And he will stand, for the Lord is able to make him stand.'

The Lordship of Christ
Thirdly, we must all submit to the Lordship of Christ. In vv. 6–9, Paul repeats the word 'Lord' seven times. He uses it like a trumpet to summon us from our self-made pedestals to the feet of Christ, to take our right place before him. If we really heeded Paul's summons we would have no difficulty in handling our disagreements with tolerance and love.

In v. 8, Paul brings the whole of human experience under the Lordship of Christ. He says, 'If we live, we live to the Lord; and if we die, we die to the Lord. So, whether we live or die, we belong to the Lord.' Our living and our dying are his business, which makes us answerable to him for our conduct, not to one another. So we should consider him in everything. We should filter the 'doubtful' things of life through such questions as, 'Can I thank God for it? Will it honour him? Will it please the Lord? Can I share it with him?'

A boy asked his girl friend to go to the cinema with him. She said, 'Could we buy three tickets?' He looked at her with astonishment. He said, 'Why would we want three tickets?' She said, 'One for the Lord Jesus!' The boy was clearly embarrassed. He said, 'I don't think the Lord Jesus would want to see the film that we're going to see.' His girl friend said, 'Then I don't want to see it either!'

For some years Charles Spurgeon, 'the Prince of Preachers', saw nothing wrong with smoking. He did not regard it as a sin. He smoked cigars in all good conscience, until he found that a tobacco firm was advertizing 'the brand that Spurgeon smokes!' From that day on he gave up the habit for he realized it was not honouring to the Lord.

In v. 9 Paul says, 'For this very reason, Christ died and returned to life so that he might be Lord of both the dead and the living.' God has made *him* our Lord across the whole range of life and death, and that frees us from what Petersen calls, 'the petty tyrannies of each other'. We must let Christ direct us through the maze of 'doubtful' things. We can certainly seek the advice of other Christians who also want to please the Lord, but we must hammer out our own convictions. We must confer with Christ and keep in step with him. In matters not dealt with specifically in the Scriptures: 'Each one should be fully convinced in his own mind' (v. 5). We must not allow other believers to foist their code of conduct on us however well meaning they might be. We must think things through for ourselves. And we must respect each other's convictions whether we agree with them or not. For as a friend said to Warren Wiersbe, 'I have learned that God blesses people I disagree with!' What a vital lesson to learn!

Paul's statement in v. 8 that 'we belong to the Lord' forms the hub of the chapter from which the spokes reach out into every part. We must bring the whole of our lives under Christ's Lordship, which means yielding to his authority, and following his directions. Then we shall enjoy the liberty we have in him, and it will not slide into licence or laxity.

Called to account

The fourth principle should certainly keep us off our self-made pedestals: we must all give an account of *ourselves* to God. That should make us think twice about finding fault with others! In v. 10, Paul confronts both the 'weak' and the 'strong' with a searching 'why?' He says to the 'weak' Christian, 'You, then, why do you judge your brother?' And he says to the 'strong' Christian, 'Why do you look down on your brother?' We all belong to the Lord so we have no right to 'judge' or 'look down' on one another. We are all answerable to him for he is the Judge, and one day we shall have to give an account of our conduct to him.

In v. 13, Paul says, 'Therefore let us stop passing judgement on one another', and the word 'Therefore' reaches back to vv. 10–12: 'For we will all stand before God's judgement seat. It is written: "As surely as I live," says the Lord, "Every knee will bow before me; every tongue will confess to God".' So then, each of us will give an account of himself to God.' It can prove dangerously distracting to keep finding fault with others, for it blinds us to our own faults. We have enough to do looking after our own lives!

The final audit

In 2 Corinthians 5:9–10, Paul shows us how to prepare for the final audit. He says, 'So we make it our goal to please him [Christ], whether we are at home in the body or away from it. For we must all appear before the judgement seat of Christ, that each one may receive what is due to him for the things done while in the body, whether good or bad.' Is *our* goal in life to please Christ? To make it that will prepare us in the best possible way for that great day when we shall have to give an account.

For 'judgement seat' Paul uses the Greek word 'bema', a word that describes the place from which the judges supervised the athletic games, and from which they gave out the rewards. So this judgement will have nothing to do with our sins, for God judged the sins of his people in Christ at Calvary. In the glorious words of Romans 8:1: 'Therefore, there is now no condemnation for those who are in Christ Jesus'. At the final audit, when Christ will go through the accounts of our lives, he will assess our works and fix our rewards. Paul lived his life against that background, and so should we. It will guard us against trying to put others right, while neglecting to examine our own attitudes and our own actions.

Liberty and love

The fifth principle links liberty with love. The 'strong' Christian rejoices in his liberty in Christ, but he should never insist on it at the expense of others. Paul makes this very clear. In one way and another he says, 'Think of others. Think of the effect that insistence on your liberty will have on them.' We must seek to help others not scorn them or judge them. We may not have the same scruples as other Christians, but we may have to limit our liberty for the sake of the 'weak'. Our liberty must be tempered by love.

Again and again Paul uses the word 'brother', and he uses it as a rebuke. In Romans 14:10 he says, 'You, then, why do you judge your brother? Or why do you look down on your brother?' In v. 13, he says, 'Make up your mind not to put any stumbling-block or obstacle in your brother's way.' In v.15, he says, 'If your brother is distressed because of what you eat, you are no longer acting in love. Do not by your eating destroy your brother for whom Christ died.' In v. 21, he says, 'It is better not to eat meat or drink wine or to do anything else that will cause your brother to fall.'

But Paul's use of the word 'brother' is more than a rebuke. It brings us into the warm, loving atmosphere of the family. It reminds us that we belong to God's Family, and that our fellow-believers are our brothers and sisters in Christ. And as in any family, some are more mature than others. Some are 'strong' but others are 'weak', and the 'strong' must help the 'weak'. As Paul puts it in 15:1: 'We who are strong ought to bear with the failings of the weak and not to please ourselves'. W.E. Vine describes these 'failings' as 'scruples which arise through weakness of faith'. The mature should always take the lead, and Paul has much to say about this. He applies this final principle in four ways, and he stamps everything he says with love.

Pleasing others

First of all, *we must resolve to please others not ourselves*. Paul puts a red line through selfishness for it has no place in the Christian life. We must use our liberty in Christ with wisdom and love. We may feel free to enjoy things that others would frown on because we have a 'strong' conscience, but we must never flaunt our freedom. It may be better at times to keep our views on these 'doubtful' things to ourselves, lest we stumble other believers. In v. 16, Paul says, 'Do not allow what you consider good to be spoken of as evil.' And in v. 22, he says, 'Whatever you believe about these things keep between yourself and God. Blessed is the man who does not condemn himself by what he approves.'

We are not dealing here with doctrine. God's people the world over, subscribe to the fundamentals of the Faith as set forth in God's Word. And we are not debating God's will for his people that he spells out in the Ten Commandments, and that are binding on all believers. We are talking about questionable things that Christians often disagree about, and we must handle such things very carefully. In v. 13, Paul urges us to turn the searchlight that we like to focus on others, on ourselves. He says, 'Therefore let us stop passing judgement on one another. Instead, make up your mind not to put any stumbling-block or obstacle in your brother's way.' We must beware of dropping banana skins that other Christians could slip on.

Paul insists that we approach this whole matter unselfishly, for our conduct in these 'doubtful' areas can have a profound effect on others. We can 'stumble' them, or cause them to fall, by riding roughshod over their scruples, and imposing our view on them. We should do the very opposite. We should defer to their conscience even if it is mistaken. We should not violate it or cause them to violate it. In 1 Corinthians 8:9, Paul says, 'Be careful … that the exercise of your freedom does not become a stumbling-block to the weak.' And we can 'distress' them, for they are easily hurt and offended. In 1 Corinthians 8:12, Paul underscores the seriousness of this. He says, 'When you sin against your brothers in this way and wound their weak conscience, you sin against Christ.' This ties in with Romans 14:15: 'If your brother is distressed because of what you eat, you are no longer acting in love.' We can even 'destroy' a fellow-believer, which means spoil his discipleship, or ruin his Christian life (Romans 14:15). And Paul drives home the seriousness of this by adding, 'For whom Christ died.' He puts this whole matter in the context of the cross.

But you may be bursting with questions at this point: 'Why should I curb my liberty just to please my brother? He may have a conscience about these questionable things, but what if I see things differently? Why should *his* conscience dictate *my* actions?' Good questions, but the way of love prompts a different question: 'Why should I use my freedom to cause somebody else to stumble?' Love gives us a deep concern for the welfare of others. As John Stott puts it, 'Love never disregards weak consciences. Love limits its own liberty out of respect for them.'

Right priorities

Secondly, *we must get our priorities right*. In v. 17, Paul says, 'For the kingdom of God is not a matter of eating and drinking, but of righteousness, peace and joy in the Holy Spirit'. The contentious issues that caused trouble amongst the Christians in Rome pale into insignificance when we set them alongside the central issues. Some were saying, 'You can eat meat that has been offered to idols and still belong to God's kingdom.' Others were saying, 'If you eat such meat you do *not* belong to God's kingdom.' They had a false view of the Christian life, and Paul corrects it.

He had to do the same when he wrote to the Christians in Corinth. In 1 Corinthians 8:8, he says, 'But food does not bring us near to God; we are no worse if we do not eat, and no better if we do.' The real issues go much deeper. The 'eternals' of 'righteousness, peace and joy in the Holy Spirit' are far more important than the 'externals' of 'eating and drinking'. Too often, like the Pharisees, we get things out of perspective.

In v. 20, Paul says, 'Do not destroy the work of God for the sake of food', and for 'food' we could read any of the 'doubtful' things that Christians disagree about. Whenever these things become an issue we should ask ourselves, 'What effect will this have on God's work? Will it help it, or hinder it? Will it build it up, or tear it down?' These are important questions, for disagreement can so easily lead to disunity. Some of God's people have sabotaged his work for things that seem so insignificant when compared with the big things of the Christian Faith. So let us put everything into this wider setting.

Pursuing peace

Thirdly, *we must pursue peace*. In v. 19, Paul says, 'Let us therefore make every effort to do what leads to peace'. The Greek word for 'make every effort' pictures a huntsman in full cry. He has his quarry in view, and he pursues it diligently. Peace in the church is that important. It is not peace at any price—we must beware of that. But we must be very sure of our ground before we make waves amongst God's people and shatter the peace.

Encouraging growth

Fourthly, *we must encourage one another to grow*. The phrase 'mutual edification' in 14:19 suggests that. I like Petersen's very practical paraphrase: 'Help others with encouraging words; don't drag them down by finding fault.' That puts the ball very firmly in our court. In 15:2, Paul says, 'Each of us should please his neighbour for his good, to build him up.'

Christian progress is like the progress of a house. How fascinating to watch it grow! It pictures what a Christian life ought to be doing. Just as a house goes up, growing against the skyline, so we should be growing nearer to God. And just as a house grows according to the plans for it, so we should grow according to the plans that God has for us in his Word. Paul wanted to see the Christians in Rome grow, so he urged the 'strong' to help the 'weak', for both need to grow. The 'strong' need to grow in patient love, so that they make allowances for the 'weak', and do not flaunt their liberty in Christ. And the 'weak' need to grow in liberating knowledge, not forever chained by a weak conscience.

The 'weak' can become 'strong', but it takes time—like the building of a house. And we must not go against our conscience however weak it is. That is the thrust of 14:23. Paul says, 'But the man who has doubts is condemned if he eats, because his eating is not from faith; and everything that does not come from faith is sin.' We must immerse ourselves in God's Word that Paul refers to in 15:4. He says, 'For everything that was written in the past was written to teach us, so that through endurance and the encouragement of the Scriptures we might have hope.' The knowledge we gain will strengthen our conscience. And we must get to grips with the big things of the Faith. Then we shall see things in perspective, and not make an issue of minor matters.

A prayer for unity

Again and again in his letters. Paul prays home the truth of what he has been teaching, and he does that here. He prays that the five principles we have been looking at might take root and bear fruit in 'a spirit of unity' amongst both the 'weak' and the 'strong'. He wanted to see peace in the church at Rome, and peace flows from unity as a quiet stream flows from a placid lake. So in 15:5–6, he prays, 'May the God who gives endurance and encouragement give you a spirit of unity among yourselves as you follow Christ Jesus, so that with one heart and mouth you may glorify the God and Father of our Lord Jesus Christ.'

I cannot forgive

Nothing blocks the flow of love like an unforgiving spirit. It pours poison into our relationships like a poisoned stream pouring into a lake. I have seen what damage it can do. Some relationships just limp along, hampered by a grudge or a grievance that lurks in the background. It has never been dealt with, and it festers like a sore. Forgiveness alone can put things right, but some people find it hard to forgive. They dig their heels in and say, 'I cannot forgive!'

Peter faced this problem head-on in Matthew 18:21. He came to Jesus and asked, 'Lord, how many times shall I forgive my brother when he sins against me? Up to seven times?' Sooner or later we all suffer at the hands of others. We cannot go through life without getting hurt. We get snubbed, or slighted, or misunderstood, or maligned, or ill-treated in some way, and then forgiveness becomes a burning issue, especially if the same person hurts us again and again. We want to hit back!

But the Lord Jesus forbids that, and if we are God's people we must live under the sceptre of his Word. In Luke 6:27–28. Jesus says, 'Love your enemies, do good to those who hate you, bless those who curse you, and pray for those who ill-treat you.' That leaves no room for grudges or grievances, but they can cling like limpets, which makes it hard to let them go. We may find it very difficult to forgive until we grasp the implication of Jesus' answer to Peter's question. That should purge every trace of an unforgiving spirit from our hearts.

The limit we set

But Peter set a limit to forgiveness, and that seems right. It finds an echo in our own hearts. Peter offered to forgive up to seven times, and he thought he was being generous. After all, the rabbis taught that twice was sufficient! For some things are very hard to forgive, and surely we cannot go on forgiving!

A survivor of one of the most brutal Nazi concentration camps, a boy who had to watch his relatives killed before his very eyes, wrote a book entitled, *I Cannot Forgive!* and we can sympathize with him. What a terrible experience! Don Cormack in his book, *Killing Fields, Living Fields* says, 'It would be a hard thing for many of the Cambodian Christians to forgive, from the heart, former Khmer Rouge, even the ones who turned to Christ, and sought to join them in the fellowships springing up in the refugee camps in Thailand.' For the Khmer Rouge carried out such terrible atrocities on their own people. Some things *are* hard to forgive.

But in Matthew 18, with startling clarity, the Lord Jesus sweeps Peter's limit aside. He brings in the arithmetic of heaven for he says, 'I tell you, not seven times, but seventy-seven times' (v. 22). In the margin it reads 'seventy times seven', an even greater number. Forgiveness on that scale makes limits and measures irrelevant, for who would count up that number of offences? With his 'seventy times seven' Jesus sets forgiveness in a very different light. He advocates a spirit of forgiveness, not just acts of forgiveness. If we are God's people, forgiveness should be worked into the very fabric of our lives. It should become a habit, for love 'keeps no record of wrongs'.

God's forgiveness

The Lord Jesus tracks this lovely flow of forgiveness to its source. He finds its spring in our relationship with God that starts with *his* forgiveness. When we open our lives to Christ in repentance and faith, God sweeps away our sins as the wind sweeps the black clouds from a stormy sky. He accepts us in his Son, the Lord Jesus Christ. He bathes our hearts in the warm sunshine of his love.

The church is the Fellowship of the Forgiven, which makes grudges and grievances in the hearts of God's people as unsightly as black ink stains on a white dress. Surely the forgiven should be forgiving!

Jesus followed his 'seventy-seven times' with one of his pictures of 'the kingdom of heaven' (v. 23). He told the story of a king who wanted to settle accounts with his servants. As he began the settlement, the king discovered that one man owed him 'ten thousand talents' (v. 24), a vast sum of money. It would probably add up to millions of pounds today. But the man had no way of settling his account so the king ordered him and his wife and children to be sold, to raise at least some of the money.

The man fell to his knees and begged for mercy. He said, 'Be patient with me … and I will pay back everything' (v. 26). What follows provides a window into the heart of God. 'The servant's master took pity on him, cancelled the debt and let him go' (v. 27). What mercy! What forgiveness! The king wiped out his servant's huge debt at a stroke, and gave him a fresh start. And that pictures God's mercy, and God's forgiveness!

Sin piles up our debt before God, for we have not given him the life we should have done. Our account is 'in the red'. Sin has laid its ravaging hand on all of us, destroying our relationship with God, and spoiling our relationships with one another. None of us have escaped its stains and chains. We have sinned in thought, word, and deed, and we have sinned at times by doing nothing. We have left so many things undone that we should have done. Forgiveness is God wiping out this huge debt for the sake of the Lord Jesus Christ. God in Christ took it to the Cross of Calvary where he paid it in full. The resurrection has been described as 'God's receipt'.

Truth in pictures

What an incredible forgiveness! The Bible uses one picture after another to bring home the wonder of it. In Psalm 103:12, David says, 'As far as the east is from the west, so far has he removed our transgressions from us.' What a vast distance! We can measure from north to south, but we cannot measure from east to west! In Isaiah 38:17, Hezekiah says to God, 'You have put all my sins behind your back.' What a lovely picture of forgiveness, for it means that God stands between us and the punishment we deserve. It points on to the Cross of Calvary. In Micah 7:19, the prophet says, 'You will … hurl all our iniquities into the depths of the sea.' And unlike some nuclear waste they will never float to the surface again. For in Hebrews 10:17, God says, 'Their sins and lawless acts I will remember no more.'

Brownlow North's ministry spanned the Revival which swept these islands in 1859, a red-letter year in the annals of church history. God greatly used him, and one day he went to speak in one of the largest churches in the city of Aberdeen. An eager congregation thronged the building, but before the service, while he was still in the vestry, Brownlow North got a letter from a man who knew his colourful past. The letter said, 'I know your past history. I followed you to Paris years ago and I know all your career of vice. I have a record of your life at Liverpool also, and I know how you carried on at Manchester. I challenge you to stand in a Christian pulpit and preach; I dare you to do it.'

Brownlow North went into the pulpit and began the service by reading that letter. He left nothing out; he read the whole letter from beginning to end. Then he said, 'My friends, it's all true, and much more besides. But I want to tell you that there came a day when God in his mercy said to me, "Brownlow North, go in peace; your sins are forgiven you", and if there is mercy for me there is mercy for you!' The service did not continue as arranged for so many people were sobbing their way to Christ.

The forgiven should be forgiving

How skilfully Jesus brings us to the punchline in his parable. The servant who had been forgiven so much went out and found a fellow servant who owed him just a few pounds. It was nothing compared with the huge debt that had been wiped from his account, but he demanded immediate payment. And he showed a heartless aggression. He grabbed the other man by the throat and he said, 'Pay back what you owe me!' (v. 28). His fellow servant responded in exactly the same way as he himself had done. He fell to his knees and begged for mercy. And he used the very words the other man had used: 'Be patient with me, and I will pay you back' (v. 29).

But the servant refused. He had the other man arrested and thrown into prison until he could pay his debt. Oh the wickedness of it! A forgiven man refusing to forgive! No wonder the other servants were outraged, and reported him to the king. For the scale of the forgiveness he had just received should have melted his heart. He should have been brimming over with gratitude. He should have been glad to share with his brother the joy of his own release. But there was nothing of that.

The way we treat others mirrors the true condition of our hearts. This man had received forgiveness but he had not appreciated it. He was just glad to be off the hook. He had not taken forgiveness into his heart, or he would have shared it. The king said to him, 'Shouldn't you have had mercy on your fellow-servant just as I had on you?' (v. 33). And in his anger the king revoked his forgiveness, and 'turned him over to the jailers to be tortured, until he should pay back all he owed' (v. 34).

Jesus made the application crystal clear. He said, 'This is how my heavenly Father will treat each of you unless you forgive your brother from your heart' (v. 35). The key phrase is 'from your heart'. The forgiven should be forgiving, for as George Herbert once said, 'He that cannot forgive others, breaks the bridge over which he must pass himself.' A forgiven life should issue in a forgiving spirit.

The cost we shun

We cannot fault the logic of forgiveness, but it can still prove very difficult. For the one who forgives is the one who suffers, and we shrink from that. We want to get our own back. In Jesus' parable the king who wiped out his servant's debt suffered the loss himself.

The cross

At the heart of all forgiveness stands a cross. We see it in God's forgiveness. It cost him the death of his own dear Son at Calvary. God offers us in Christ a full and free forgiveness for all our sins, but his forgiveness is not cheap. Christ *died* that we might be forgiven. In 1 John 2:12, the apostle writes, 'Your sins have been forgiven on account of his name.' Every act of divine forgiveness is written in the blood of Jesus. The one who forgives is the one who suffers.

We see it in man's forgiveness, but we find this cross hard to accept. When we get hurt we want to get even. This desire lies deeply embedded in our hearts, and ill-treatment brings it to the surface. If others make us suffer we want to make them suffer in return. Forgiveness seems unjust and unfair. As Charles Swindoll puts it, 'Most of us would rather sit on a judgement seat than a mercy seat. If somebody 'did us wrong', we'd rather watch him squirm in misery than smile in relief.'

And little things, not just big things, can provoke this longing for revenge It may not be some outrageous offence; it may be a snub, or a bit of sarcasm, or some deliberate wound to our pride. Now what happens when we forgive? We suffer without hitting back. We absorb the hurt in our own hearts.

When Thomas Barnardo, who founded Barnardos' Homes, was a medical student in East London, he got involved in a riot in a public house. He had gone in to sell Bibles, but the drunken ruffians inside attacked him with great fury and flung him to the ground. Then they grabbed a table and put it, legs upward, on his prostrate body, and began to jump up and down on it. When Barnardo was taken unconscious to his lodgings, he was bruised from head to foot, and had some broken ribs.

Six weeks passed before he was up and about again. Of course the police intervened, and they urged Barnardo to prosecute the ringleaders, but he refused. He said, 'I've begun with the Gospel, and I'm determined not to the end with the Law.' The one who forgives is the one who suffers.

Just recently a newspaper headline grabbed my attention: 'This true Christian has a gift for mercy'. It went on to tell the story of Jo Pollard, who added the names of the three men convicted of murdering her husband to her Christmas list. He was killed when the couple were robbed while delivering aid to a Romanian hospital. She says she has forgiven the men responsible, and has visited them in prison. She has also parcelled up books, calendars and paintings of her native Yorkshire and sent them with love. She also wishes them the happiest Christmas. Jo Pollard suffered without hitting back. She absorbed the hurt in her own heart. The one who forgives is the one who suffers.

I believe that forgiveness forms part of the cross that the Lord Jesus thrusts into the path of his would-be disciples. In Luke 14:27, he says, 'And anyone who does not carry his cross and follow me cannot be my disciple.' If we dig our heels in and refuse to forgive we evade this cross, which makes discipleship impossible.

In 1 Peter 3:8–9, the apostle shows us how to live in harmony with one another and amongst other things he says, in Eugene Petersen's paraphrase, 'No retaliation. No sharp-tongued sarcasm. Instead bless—that's your job, to bless. You'll be a blessing and also get a blessing.' This ties in with the English proverb: 'Forgiveness and a smile are the best form of revenge.' But a cross runs through that, for the one who forgives is the one who suffers. We absorb the hurt without trying to get even. What a lovely way to short-circuit some of the evil in the world!

We see how perfectly the Lord Jesus portrayed this way of life in 1 Peter 2:23–24. 'When they hurled their insults at him, he did not retaliate; when he suffered, he made no threats. Instead, he entrusted himself to him who judges justly. He himself bore our sins in his body on the tree'. And Jesus blazed this trail for us to follow. For two verses earlier, the apostle tells us that Jesus left us an example, 'that you should follow in his steps'. Then he shows us how the Lord's steps led to Calvary, to the cruel cross with all its hurt and pain. And he directs *us* down this path, but we can only follow it as we live in daily partnership with the Lord Jesus, the Christ of Calvary. We must keep our lives open to him, for he alone can draw the poison of anger and bitterness from our hearts.

The cost of an unforgiving spirit

If we refuse to forgive others because we reject the cross, we do not escape suffering. We condemn ourselves to a greater torment, for instead of absorbing the hurt and moving on, we hammer the nail of hurt in more deeply. We prolong the pain. It is like having a piercing thorn embedded in the finger and refusing to have it taken out. If we plan revenge on those who have wronged us we punish ourselves far more than we punish them. In Jesus' parable the unforgiving servant put himself into the hands of 'the torturers'.

An unforgiving spirit hardens us. It puts us in a prison of bitterness and misery. Jesus pictures this prison in his parable. The king at first had mercy on his servant and saved him from prison, but by refusing to forgive his fellow servant he put himself back in. He languished in a prison of his own making. Some of the most miserable people are those who will not forgive others. The forgiven should be forgiving for their sakes as well as for the sake of others.

The pattern we are shown

In Ephesians 4:22, 24, Paul urges us to dress from the right wardrobe. He says, 'put off your old self', as you would strip off dirty clothes, for no Christian should be seen in 'clothes' from this wardrobe. We must dress from the new wardrobe that God has given us in Christ. A Christian man came down to breakfast in a foul temper, and started snapping at his wife. She said to him, 'You have the old man's shirt on this morning!' He had dressed from the wrong wardrobe! Paul says, 'put on the new self', and he shows us how to be properly dressed, especially in our relationships with others.

He shows us the sort of things to strip off because they belong to the old wardrobe, things like lying, stealing, bitterness, malice, and foul talk. He includes wrath, which can blow up in a moment, and anger, which can have a slower fuse. All these things spoil our relationships. They have no place in the Christian life.

And Paul shows us some of the lovely things we must put on, things that belong to our new wardrobe in Christ. In 4:32, he says, 'Be kind and compassionate to one another, forgiving each other, just as in Christ God forgave you.' Forgiveness in relationships is so important because we are so imperfect. The closer we get to one another, the more likely we are to hurt one another. Fellowship depends on forgiveness.

And Paul tells us plainly what kind of forgiveness he has in mind—'just as in Christ God forgave you'. In Jesus' parable the king's forgiveness provided a lovely pattern for the servant's own forgiveness, but sadly he rejected it. Things would have been so different if he had treated his fellow servant as he himself had been treated, but he hardened his heart. And in 5:1–2, God's forgiveness clearly provides a pattern for our forgiveness, and Paul anchors it in our hearts with a strong 'Therefore'. He says, 'Be imitators of God, therefore, as dearly loved children and live a life of love, just as Christ loved us and gave himself up for us'. And the word 'imitators' commits us to a pattern not just a path.

No reluctance

I like Eugene Petersen's paraphrase of 4:32: 'Forgive one another as quickly and thoroughly as God in Christ forgave you.' How freely and fully God has forgiven us, if we are his people. We detect no hint of reluctance in his forgiveness so we should harbour no reluctance in ours. We should forgive from our hearts.

The American preacher, Ronald Dunn, in a message given at The Keswick Convention in 1978 on 'Moving Mountains', suggests that whether we know it or not we all carry a little black book around with us. In it we keep all the 'I.O.U.s we are holding against people. He says, 'You know how it is. "I'm holding an I.O.U. against Mrs Jones for what she said about me." "I'm holding an I.O.U. against the pastor because he didn't call on me." You know what forgiveness is? It's tearing those I.O.U.s up and saying,

"They don't owe me a thing. They may have wronged me, they may have harmed me, but I forgive, I forgive, I forgive."'

We have received that kind of forgiveness from God. He does not say, 'I'll forgive you, but I want nothing more to do with you!' Or, 'I'll forgive you, but I don't want you in my home!' Or 'I'll forgive you, but don't expect me to be your friend!' God grants us in Christ a free pardon and the opportunity of a new life. '"Come now, let us reason together", says the Lord, "Though your sins are like scarlet, they shall be as white as snow; though they are red as crimson, they shall be like wool"' (Isaiah 1:18). Sin stains, and God in Christ has provided us with a wonderful stain remover. 1 John 1:7 says, 'the blood of Jesus, his Son, purifies us from all sin.'

No reserve

David begins Psalm 103 with an anthem of praise, and he calls on all that is within him to join the choir. He cries, 'Praise the Lord, O my soul; all my inmost being, praise his holy name.' He wants his whole personality to be caught up in a great song of thanksgiving. And he picks out some of the things that have stirred him so much, including forgiveness. He says, 'Praise the Lord, O my soul … Who forgives all your sins'.

Mark the word 'all'. God does not say to us, 'I'll forgive this sin, but I will not forgive that sin.' It is '*all* your sins'. Many Christians have found assurance in that little word 'all'. Maybe a particular sin has preyed on our minds because it has seemed unforgivable. We have tortured ourselves about it, but then God has lit up this 'all' of forgiveness, and it has become a grave in which we have buried all our doubts. What a theme for praise! And what a pattern for our forgiveness! We, too, must forgive without reluctance and without reserve.

Should forgiveness be unconditional?

But what if there is no repentance? What if the person who has hurt us refuses to say sorry? Helmut Thielicke, a German who lived through the horrors of Nazism, confronts this problem in his book *The Waiting Father not just Waiting*. He says, 'This business of forgiving is by no means a simple thing … We say, "Very well, if the other fellow is sorry and begs my pardon, I will forgive him …" We make of forgiveness a law of reciprocity. And this never works. For then both of us say to ourselves, "The other fellow has to make the first move". And then I watch like a hawk to see whether the other person will flash a signal to me with his eyes or whether I can detect some small hint between the lines of his letter which shows that he is sorry. I am always on the point of forgiving ... but I never forgive. I am far too just.'

The only remedy, as Thielicke discovered, is to follow the pattern of God's forgiveness, which puts the ball into our court. We must take the initiative, as God took the initiative in the Gospel. Jesus illustrated that in his parables of grace, as Philip Yancey points out in his book *What's So Amazing About Grace*. He describes God as, 'A lovesick father who runs to meet the prodigal, a landlord who cancels a debt too large for any servant to reimburse, an employer who pays eleventh-hour workers the same as the first-hour crew, a banquet-giver who goes out to the highways and byways in search of undeserving guests.' All this may seem to defy the natural law of retribution and fairness, but as Yancey puts it, 'Calvary broke up the logjam between justice and forgiveness.' For at the Cross, God's Son absorbed within himself all the demands of justice, that he might dispense God's forgiving grace. And we see again that the one who forgives is the one who suffers.

God in his grace did not leave us undisturbed in our sins, with no possibility of forgiveness. This truth lies at the very heart of the Gospel. And just as God made the first move, so must we. We are to forgive each other 'just as in Christ God forgave you'. If the move we make fails to get a response there can be no reconciliation, for it takes a sincere 'Sorry' to restore fellowship. But at least it will drain the poison of resentment and bitterness from our hearts, and release a flow of love for those who have hurt us. And this ties in with the exhortations in Romans 12:18,21: 'If it is possible, as far as it depends on you, live at peace with everyone ... Do not be overcome by evil, but overcome evil with good.'

Learn to forget

In Hebrews 8, we find the great provisions of the New Covenant that God has made with his people in Christ, and v.12 describes his superlative forgiveness: 'For I will forgive their wickedness and will remember their sins no more.' God forgives and forgets. How wonderful yet how challenging, for again we have to pattern our forgiveness on God's! You might say, 'I'll forgive but I cannot forget.' It is not easy, for resentment can sink deep into our hearts, but with the Lord's help it is possible.

For we have a greater control over remembering and forgetting than many of us realize. We have to make an effort to remember, and repetition plays a big part. We have to go over the same thing again and again. If we want to forget we must reverse the process. When the hurt, or the injury, or the disloyalty floods back into our minds we must build a dam against it. We must resolve to forget. We must think about something else, something that will grip our minds and turn them into other channels, and we must repeat the process again and again. We may never forget the facts for they will have deep roots, but the bitterness will fade, and we shall be able to cope.

When I was a student in London, Dr Sangster was minister of the Central Hall, Westminster. He was having a fruitful ministry, but he had his critics like most ministers. And one Christmas, one of his guests, who had come a few days early, saw him sending off the last of his Christmas cards. He was startled to see a certain name and address. 'Surely, you are not sending a greeting to *him*,' he said. 'Why not?' asked Sangster. 'But you remember,' he began, eighteen months ago …'

Dr Sangster says, 'I remembered, then, the thing this man had publicly said about me, but I remembered also resolving at the time, that with God's help, I would remember to forget. And God had made me forget!'

He posted the card.

God's power

We can only follow God's pattern of forgiveness as we open our lives to his love and power. With his help we can forgive as freely and fully as he does, but *only* with his help. And we can even forgive and forget! We naturally hang on to grudges and grievances, for we want to pay others back in their own coin. But God's forgiveness, really received, changes all that. We cannot withhold forgiveness from others when God has so graciously forgiven us.

Mending the fences

When Paul wrote his letter to the Philippians he dipped his pen constantly into the ink of love. But he had more than a human love for them. He says, 'God can testify how I long for you all with the affection of Christ Jesus' (Philippians 1:8). By the ministry of God's Spirit, Paul had been infused with the love of Christ and it overflowed to other believers, especially to those in Philippi with whom he was very close. In 4:1, he calls them his 'dear friends', and tells them how much he loves them and longs for them. And whenever he thought about them praise welled up from deep in his heart, and he would pour it out in his prayers for them. He was particularly grateful for their ongoing partnership in the gospel. They had contributed to his support again and again, and he wrote to tell them how grateful he was.

Indeed, the church at Philippi had the distinction of being in Paul's heart, and he tells them that. He says, 'I have you in my heart' (1:7). What a great place to be! They were on his mind, for he would often think about them. They were on his prayer list, for he would often pray for them. And they were on his lips, for he would often talk about them. But best of all they were in his heart, and that gave him a deep concern for them that comes out in his letter.

Letters are like telephone conversations; if we listen in, we can only hear one side of them. So when we read Paul's letters we have to read between the lines. And it becomes clear that one thing in particular made him very uneasy, as we saw in a previous chapter. Broken relationships in the church were posing a serious threat to their unity. In 1:27, he says, 'Whatever happens, conduct yourselves in a manner worthy of the gospel of Christ. Then, whether I come and see you or only hear about you in my absence, I will know that you stand firm in one spirit, contending as one man for the faith of the gospel.' Paul wanted them to present a united front, like a military march-past with not a shoulder out of place!

Unity not uniformity

What a lovely picture of a local church! Would that every church matched up to it, for this is where unity must begin. In his book, *Joy Way,* Guy King puts this picture on a bigger canvas. He has the wider church in mind, and he says, 'There may be different regiments—call them, if you will, Anglicans, Congregationalists, Baptists, Brethren, Methodists, Presbyterians, and so on—but it is the same army, facing the same enemy, in the same Cause, under the same Commander.' What a helpful way of thinking of the various denominations! We may have our differences, but if we have been born of God's Spirit, and we know the joy of God's forgiveness through the cross, and we have a living practical faith in Jesus Christ as the crucified, risen, living, exalted Saviour, we have so much in common.

But we must not confuse unity with uniformity, which has the word *uniform* in it. That suggests dressing alike, sounding alike, thinking alike, and acting alike. But that is not biblical unity, for Paul's picture of the church as a body rules uniformity right out of court. In 1 Corinthians 12, he says, 'If the whole body were an eye, where would the sense of hearing be? If the whole body were an ear, where would the sense of smell be? But in fact God has arranged the parts in the body, every one of them, just as he wanted them to be. If they were all one part, where would the body be? As it is, there are many parts, but one body' (vv. 17–20).

Uniformity comes from outside and can be imposed, but unity comes from inside, from sharing a common life. And it comes from a right attitude to one another. We may not agree on everything, but we can still enjoy harmony in the church. For our unity in Christ, like the unity of the body, is unity in variety. In his book, *Laugh Again,* Charles Swindoll describes it as 'the inner desire to conduct oneself in a cooperative manner ... to be on the same team, to go for the same objective, for the benefit of one another.'

Incentives and imperatives

Paul pursues this theme of unity in Philippians 2:2 with a personal plea. He says, 'Make my joy complete by being like-minded, having the same love, being one in spirit and purpose.' And he sandwiches his plea between incentives and imperatives, between things that promote unity, and things that destroy it.

Paul begins with a cluster of incentives, and he finds them all in Christ.

He says, 'If you have any encouragement from being united with Christ, if any comfort from his love, if any fellowship with the Spirit, if any tenderness and compassion …' (v. 1). All these things move in the direction of unity not discord. They nip disharmony very firmly in the bud. We cannot take such things on board and remain at loggerheads with fellow-believers.

Paul strengthens his plea with a cluster of imperatives, and he centres them all on the old self that threatens all of us. He says, 'Do nothing out of selfish ambition or vain conceit, but in humility consider others better than yourselves. Each of you should look not only to your own interests, but also to the interests of others' (vv. 3–4). For what damage the old self can do in the fellowship of the church! It can destroy every trace of unity. Paul alerts us to the danger, and puts us on our guard.

Paul had such a close relationship with the Philippians that he could make his plea very personal. He says, 'Make my joy complete by being like-minded'. Discord divides and brings nothing but dismay, but harmony brings happiness. And how discord hinders the spread of the gospel, for it distracts the church from its missionary task, and turns it in upon itself. It would make such a difference to Paul himself if the Christians at Philippi were truly united, standing shoulder to shoulder in the defence and proclamation of the gospel.

Euodia and Syntyche

So far Paul has been pleading for unity in the church as a whole, and that should have been enough. God's people should have applied his Word to themselves, and used it to examine their own relationships, but how slow we are to do that! We have all sorts of ways of evading the thrust of God's Word! We find it too personal, or too humbling, or too difficult. So it lies uselessly in our minds, like lumber stored away in an attic, and it has no effect at all on our lives.

Paul recognizes this, so in 4:2–3, he becomes very specific. Naming names he singles out two of the women in the church and says, 'I plead with Euodia and I plead with Syntyche to agree with each other in the Lord.' All sorts of speculations have been made about these two women, but we have no other mention of them so we know very little about them.

But Paul knew them well, and he had fond memories of them. He says, '[they] have contended at my side in the cause of the gospel' (v. 3). He does not give us any details, but he recalls their close involvement with him in the work. They had not just stood on the sidelines. How encouraging to have fellow-Christians at our side to help us in God's work! Maybe like Lydia they were businesswomen who had prominence and influence in the church.

But now they had fallen out, and Paul urges them to put their relationship right. For if they allowed their quarrel to drag on it would fester like a sore, and the trouble would spread. People would take sides and the situation would get steadily worse. How often that has happened! Because the conflict has not been dealt with, minor irritations have developed into major disputes, and tiny squalls have blown up into fierce storms. Clashes and skirmishes amongst God's people have been allowed to muddy the waters of church life over and over again.

Not that all conflicts are wrong. Sometimes we have to dig our heels in and fight for the preservation of the truth. Paul had to do that more than once to guard the purity of the gospel, as we shall see in another chapter. But too often disagreements in the church, like the quarrel between Euodia and Syntyche, flow from stubbornness and selfishness, like water from a polluted spring. And Paul shows us how to deal with them, and we need his help, for all the while 'depravity pollutes humanity' disagreements will occur however much we try to avoid them.

Paul's approach

Paul approaches Euodia and Syntyche through the door of v.1 that swings open on the hinges of love. He makes a plea to the whole church. He says, 'Therefore, my brothers, you whom I love and long for, my joy and crown … stand firm in the Lord, dear friends!'

See how Paul expresses his own attitude to other Christians, for apostolic attitudes are Christian ideals. He had a deep affection for them that comes out in the very words he uses. He describes them as 'you whom I love and long for', and he calls them his 'dear friends'. Let us not miss the thrust of this for our own hearts. For if this is the way Christians should view each other it makes broken relationships in the church for selfish reasons, a scandal. If they can be restored they should be, as quickly as possible. What a challenge to Euodia and Syntyche—and to us!

And Paul addresses them all as 'my brothers', a reminder of the true nature of the church. When God saves us he adopts us into his Family, which makes us brothers and sisters in Christ. That should surely make a difference to the way we treat one another. Any breakdown in our relationships spoils the quality of our church life, for how can we worship, or work, or witness together helpfully and effectively if disagreements are tearing us apart?

I knew a couple who had the husband's father, who was a widower, living with them, and each Sunday they attended their local church and worshipped together. They would kneel side by side and as God's children repeat the Family Prayer. But God sees everything, and he saw the chasm that separated them. For at home the wife resented her father-in-law and made his life a misery. She constantly found fault with him. How that tainted their worship! It must grieve our Heavenly Father to see his children at loggerheads! What a wise approach Paul made to Euodia and Syntyche!

He also addresses them all as 'my joy and crown'. What a lovely way to view our fellow-Christians! Paul found 'joy' in the Christians at Philippi because they meant so much to him. Love and joy walk hand in hand. And in a special way they were his 'crown' for he had seen many of them come to Christ. And the crown he refers to was not the 'diadema' crown of royalty but the 'stephanos' crown of victory. It was given to successful athletes in the Games. So Paul saw the Philippian Christians as evidences of battles fought and victories won. What a helpful way to view our fellow-believers! For it reminds us that we fight in a much bigger conflict than any conflict we might know amongst ourselves. We should watch out for *the* enemy not treat one another as enemies.

Stand firm

Paul climaxes v. 1 by urging every Christian in Philippi to 'stand firm in the Lord'. What a vital command! We see that from the way Paul repeats it in other letters. He says to the Corinthians, 'Be on your guard; stand firm in the faith' (1 Corinthians 16:13). He says to the Galatians, 'It is for freedom that Christ has set us free. Stand firm, then' (Galatians 5:1). And he says to the Thessalonians, 'So then, brothers, stand firm and hold to the teachings we passed on to you' (2 Thessalonians 2:15).

But in his command to the Philippians Paul adds a very significant phrase—'in the Lord'. We must be 'rooted ... in *him*', as Colossians 2:7 puts it. Just as a towering tree puts its roots deep into the soil, so we too must put the roots of our faith deep into Christ. That alone is the secret of steadfastness. We shall never stand firm in our own strength. We need the Lord's help in everything, for this is not a God-friendly world.

Look at that mighty oak standing firm amidst the howling winds. It takes hold of the earth, but even more important, the earth takes hold of the tree. It is not just we, but he! So we must stand firm *in him*, as a tree stands firm in the soil. We must root our confidence in him for he will never fail us. And by faith and prayer we must draw on *his* resources. 'Please Lord, your strength'—'your love'—'your peace'—'your joy'—or whatever else we need.

Paul's personal plea

Having prepared the way, Paul turns immediately to Euodia and Syntyche. He uses Philippians 4:1 as a springboard to launch a personal plea to them. For standing firm in the Lord includes loving his people, and living in harmony with them. We cannot 'stand firm' unless we stand together. The winds of discord and disharmony will soon blow us off course. So in v. 2, Paul says, 'I plead with Euodia and I plead with Syntyche to agree with each other ...'

How embarrassing for these women that Paul should single them out, and for such a reason! But he took a serious view of this rift between them, so, first of all, *he made it public*. For when two members of the church fall out it can affect the whole church. It is not just a private matter.

For church membership is body membership, not club membership. As Paul puts it in Ephesians 4:25: 'we are all members of one body.' People gather in clubs because they have a common interest. Club membership involves paying an annual subscription, attending meetings, and having the right to vote. But church membership is very different, for in Christ we have a common life, not just a common interest. We belong to one another like members of a human body, so broken relationships harm the body life of the church. We betray the unity and trust that should bind us together, and knit our hearts in Christ.

A cry from the heart

So Paul makes this quarrel between Euodia and Syntyche public, for his letter would be read to the whole church. That underscores its seriousness. And then, secondly, *he appeals to them from his heart*. He says, 'I plead with Euodia and I plead with Syntyche'. As an apostle he could have pulled rank, he could have insisted on a reconciliation, he could have warned them or threatened them. But Paul had a deep knowledge of the human heart. He knew that it takes more than apostolic commands to restore broken relationships, so he pleads with these women. He reaches out to them in love, for love alone will melt stubborn, selfish hearts. And he uses the Greek word *parakaleo*, the verb that lies behind 'Paraclete' the name that Jesus gave to the Holy Spirit. How significant! The word means literally 'one who is called alongside' to help. It has the ideas of comfort and encouragement in it. It means to beg, to exhort, to implore. What a lovely word to use! Paul pours his heart into it, and his approach allies him with the Holy Spirit.

Both parties

Thirdly, *Paul pleads with both parties*. He says, 'I plead with Euodia and I plead with Syntyche'. He did not side with either of them; neither did he discuss the details of their quarrel. He spoke to each woman alike, for when a relationship breaks down there are usually faults on both sides. I have seen very few exceptions to this, for the road to such a breakdown is seldom a one-way street! But no doubt both Euodia and Syntyche said, 'I'm right, she's wrong', for we tend to build entrenched positions and then defend them vigorously. It takes a good dose of humility to ask, 'Am *I* in the wrong?' But to Paul each was under the same obligation to make the first move. Neither was to wait for the other. We saw the importance of this in a previous chapter. We may even have to make a conditional apology: 'I don't see where I've wronged you, but it's clear that you feel I've hurt you, so please forgive me.' What a challenge to us if we have broken relationships!

In the Lord

Then, as Paul continues to urge Euodia and Syntyche towards harmony, *he appeals to them on the right ground*. He pleads with them 'to agree with each other in the Lord', or as J.B. Phillips paraphrases it: 'I beg you … to make up your differences as Christians should.' Paul wanted them to deal with their dispute as fellow-believers, to bring the resources of Christ to bear on it.

The phrase 'in the Lord' brings *him* into it, and sets it in a new light. Jesus Christ is Lord, and the very phrase 'in the Lord' should bring us to his feet in submission and surrender. It challenged these women to yield themselves and their relationship to him. It gave them a new focus for their grievances. It urged them to focus on the Lord Jesus and what they shared in him. They were both in God's family, so they were sisters in Christ. They should be saying to themselves, 'She is my sister', and that should give them the incentive to put things right.

They needed help

Paul has surely said enough to heal the breach between Euodia and Syntyche, but he takes nothing for granted. He knows how slow we can be to do the right thing. So next *he seeks help for them*. He leaves no stone unturned to bring about reconciliation. He says, 'Yes, and I ask you, loyal yoke-fellow, help these women …' He calls for a third party to arbitrate between them, for he can only look on from a distance. He wants somebody on the spot to help them iron out their differences. This is no easy task, as I know from experience, for it demands love, and tact, and a complete lack of prejudice. But sometimes it needs to be done for the good of the church.

Paul does not identify the 'loyal yoke-fellow' so we can only speculate about him. Various names have been suggested—Luke, Barnabas, Timothy, Silas—but his name is far less important than the 'help' he could give. And the Greek word that Paul uses is quite a mouthful! It is *sunantilambanomi*. It means literally 'to take hold of together with opposite'. We have all seen illustrations of it. We could picture it as two people moving a table from one room to another, carrying it together, and taking opposite sides.

We find the same word in the story of Martha and Mary in Luke 10.

Martha welcomes Jesus into her home and works really hard to prepare a good meal for him. She wanted to do her very best. We can imagine her bustling around the kitchen, putting the vegetables on, basting the meat, and looking for her best dishes. She wanted to get everything ready for the proper time, but she had so much to do, and she had only one pair of hands. If only Mary would lend a hand! But she was with Jesus drinking in his word, and he seemed to be encouraging her. Martha got more and more irritated and exasperated, and in the end she boiled over. She stormed out of the kitchen and said, 'Lord, don't you care that my sister has left me to do the work by myself? Tell her to help me!' (v. 40). *Sunantilambanomi!* Martha did not want Mary to do all the work; she wanted them to do it together.

We also find the same word in Romans 8:26. Paul says, 'We do not know what we ought to pray for', and we can all identify with that problem. We run into it again and again like a motorist in a built-up area, meeting a string of red traffic lights. But God has given us a Partner in prayer, the Holy Spirit. Paul says, 'the Spirit helps us in our weakness'. *Sunantilambanomi!* What an encouragement! That explains Paul's reference to praying in the Spirit in Ephesians 6:18. He says, 'And pray in the Spirit on all occasions with all kinds of prayers and requests.' The Holy Spirit does not leave us to carry the burden of prayer on our own. He takes one side, we take the other, and we carry it together. As we play our part, the Holy Spirit will play his. We can count on his co-operation.

All this lights up the kind of help Paul wanted his 'loyal yoke-follow' to give Euodia and Syntyche. He wanted him to bring them together and to encourage them to listen to each other's point of view, and they needed that encouragement. For too often, when relationships break down, we refuse to listen. We are so sure that we are right that we want to do all the talking! We want to justify *ourselves*, and to put *our* view of things.

A willingness to listen could break the deadlock. We may have been wronged but there may have been a reason for that. Being humble enough to listen could be the first step to releasing our grievances, imagined or real, and offering our forgiveness. In this way we follow in the steps of the Lord Jesus who, 'When they hurled their insults at him, he did not retaliate; when he suffered, he made no threats. Instead, he entrusted himself to him who judges justly' (1 Peter 2:23). So Paul says to his friend, 'help these women'. Lead them through the desert of their dispute to an oasis of harmony and peace.

Do not write them off

Next, Paul had *some good things* to say about Euodia and Syntyche. He gives them both an impressive CV. He says, they 'have contended at my side in the cause of the gospel, along with Clement and the rest of my fellow-workers' (v. 3). For 'contended' Paul uses the Greek word *sunathleo* that means, 'to strive', like an athlete striving for victory in the Games. So these women had worked really hard with Paul as he had sought to spread the gospel. They had given him their wholehearted support. They belonged to a band of helpers who had been a great encouragement to Paul.

But how easy it is, when trouble arises between two people in the church, to write them off! Such trouble can act like a rubber to erase good things in the past. So Paul reminds the Christians at Philippi that Euodia and Syntyche had done a lot of good. They had been his colleagues, and they were two he could count on. They had fallen out, yes, but Paul wanted no one to forget their record of service. Whatever had gone wrong he wanted *that* to count in their favour, for he had really appreciated their help. So he put the whole thing into perspective.

The book of life

Finally, whatever the church's attitude to Euodia and Syntyche, *God had not written them off!* For Paul says that their names, along with Clement's and the rest of Paul's fellow-workers, 'are in the book of life'. What an important 'book'! Nothing brings that home like the scenes of judgement in Revelation 20. John sees the dead, small and great, judged out of the books that are opened. He says, 'The dead were judged according to what they had done as recorded in the books' (v. 12). God knows everything we have thought, said, or done, so the verdict 'Guilty!' rings out again and again as the 'books' expose what people have tried to hide.

But John says, 'Another book was opened, which is the book of life' (v. 12). In this 'book' God has inscribed the names of all his people, people like Euodia, Syntyche, Clement, and all the rest. Paul himself had his name in this 'book'. Have you? Revelation 21:27 describes it as 'the *Lamb's* book of life' which helps us to identify God's people. They are those who believe that the Lord Jesus Christ is God's Sacrificial Lamb.

1 Peter 3:18 says, 'Christ died for sins once for all, the righteous for the unrighteous, to bring you to God.' And then he vindicated him by raising him from the dead. Jesus Christ is victoriously and vibrantly alive! God's people are those who have pinned all their hopes on him, for this life and the next. They trust him, love him, follow him, and serve him. Without the Lord Jesus we have no hope, for Revelation 20:15 says, 'If anyone's name was not found written in the book of life, he was thrown into the lake of fire.' What a terrible fate! Make sure that *your* name is in this 'book'.

One day Jesus sent out some of his disciples two by two, to prepare the way for him, and they came back rejoicing that even the demons were subject to them! They revelled in their newfound power. But Jesus said to them, 'Do not rejoice that the spirits submit to you, but rejoice that your names are written in heaven' (Luke 10:20)—for nothing matters more than that. And the Greek verb 'written', which is in the perfect tense, means that they will never be erased! Once he has truly saved us God will never write us off!

The name of Jesus

Do you have fences to mend in your relationships? Then I urge you in the name of Jesus to start the repair work as soon as possible. If you find it difficult think long and hard about him, for as Charles Swindoll puts it—in his book, *Laugh Again*—'There is something magnanimous about the name of Jesus that softens our attitude and defuses disharmony. Somehow the insertion of his name makes it inappropriate to maintain a fighting spirit.' And he underscores this truth with a telling story from the life of Charles Spurgeon, the famous Baptist preacher who ministered in London in the 19th century.

Spurgeon had a pastor-friend, Dr Newman Hall, who wrote a book entitled *Come to Jesus*. Another preacher published an article in which he ridiculed Hall, who bore it patiently for a while. But when the article gained popularity, Hall sat down and wrote a letter of protest. His answer was full of retaliatory invectives that outdid anything in the article that attacked him. Before posting the letter, Hall took it to Spurgeon for his opinion.

Chapter 9

Spurgeon read it carefully then, handing it back, said it was excellent and that the writer of the article deserved it all. 'But,' he added, 'it just lacks one thing.' After a pause Spurgeon continued, 'Underneath your signature you ought to write the words, "Author of *Come to Jesus*".'

The two godly men looked at each other for a few minutes. Then Hall tore the letter to shreds.

Love's intolerance

When love clashes with the harsh realities of life we see it in a different light. It will lean over backwards to be kind and helpful to those in need, but it will not tolerate things that threaten others' welfare. Its very concern makes it intolerant at times. We see this in the life of the Lord Jesus.

One day, just before the Passover, he stood in the outer court of the Temple looking round at the merchants and moneychangers, who had turned the place into a shopping mall. They sold cattle, sheep and doves for sacrifice, and changed money for those who wanted to pay the Temple tax. Business was brisk as they raked in their exorbitant profits. What Jesus saw made him so angry that he made a whip out of some thongs that the cattle drivers used, and with stern look and flashing eye he drove those traders from the Temple.

We can just imagine the scene, for what mayhem Jesus caused! He stampeded the sheep and oxen and overturned the tables of the moneychangers, scattering their coins in every direction! To the men who were selling doves he said, 'Get these out of here! How dare you turn my Father's house into a market!' (John 2:16). He was like a ball of fire! His words scorched the traders' hearts and sent them scurrying like rats to the nearest exit. With their greed and exploitation they had turned 'a house of prayer' into 'a den of robbers', making religion serve their own selfish ends instead of the purposes of God. And they ruined it for so many people. Jesus' reaction made his disciples think of a verse in the Psalms: 'Zeal for your house consumes me' (Psalm 69:9).

But many people find this story disturbing because they cannot fit it into their picture of Jesus. They regard him as the most loving person who has ever lived, as 'gentle Jesus, meek and mild'. To see him with a whip in his hand, chasing men from the Temple courts, seems so out of character. But this was not the only time that Jesus showed his anger.

Stubborn hearts

One day, in the synagogue in Capernaum, the Pharisees felt the heat of it, for it burned against them. It was the Sabbath, and as Jesus looked round the congregation his roving eye picked out a man with a shrivelled hand. The Pharisees knew Jesus' reputation so they watched him closely to see if he would heal the man. For in their book, that would violate their jealously guarded regulations for Sabbath-keeping.

Jesus knew their hearts so he deliberately put the man in the spotlight. He got him to stand up in front of everyone. Then he asked them, 'Which is lawful on the Sabbath: to do good or to do evil, to save life or to kill?' (Mark 3:4). They just sat and scowled at him, and as Jesus looked round at them his eyes blazed with anger. How dare they put their own rigid rules before the welfare of this man with the shrivelled hand!

Mark says that Jesus was 'deeply distressed at their stubborn hearts' (v. 5). So there was grief as well as granite in his anger. He was distressed for *them* because they had hardened religion down into a burdensome list of restrictions and regulations. And they had dried up the springs of compassion in their own hearts. What a tragedy! But Jesus could not tolerate their attitude, so he delayed the man's healing no longer. In front of everyone he said, 'Stretch out your hand', and Mark says, 'He stretched it out, and his hand was completely restored' (v. 5). What a miracle! But it cut no ice with the Pharisees. Mark says they 'went out and began to plot with the Herodians how they might kill Jesus' (v. 6).

The little children

And even his disciples knew the lash of his indignation! It happened on a day when many parents crowded around Jesus because they wanted him to touch their children. They wanted his blessing on them as we want his blessing on our children today. But the disciples, like self-appointed bodyguards, pushed them away none too kindly. Maybe they wanted to protect Jesus from too many demands on his time and strength. Or maybe they thought he was too busy to spend time on the children. Whatever the reason, it put them out of step with Jesus and they ran full tilt into his anger. His eyes flashed with indignation at such a breach of love, for he wanted to gather the children around him. He said to the disciples, 'Let the little children come to me, and do not hinder them, for the kingdom of God belongs to such as these' (Mark 10:14).

For the sake of others

Love, then, has limits to its tolerance, not for its own sake, but for the sake of others. The Lord Jesus never got angry for himself. Men heaped insults on him, they slandered him, they mocked him, and they falsely accused him. But he never showed a trace of anger. And how they ill-treated him! They spat in his face, they pulled his beard, they whipped him with a scourge, and then they nailed him to a cross. But he never showed a trace of anger. Even when the soldiers were driving the nails through his hands and feet he cried, 'Father, forgive them, for they do not know what they are doing' (Luke 23:34).

Jesus' anger had no selfishness in it. He directed it against those who were hurting others, and exploiting the helpless and the weak. It blazed against the traders in the Temple, who were more interested in money than men, and who were using religion to line their own pockets. It burned against the Pharisees, who in their warped state of mind thought that *their* petty rules of Sabbath-keeping were more important than the welfare of men. And it flamed against the disciples when they tried to keep the children from him. How could they discount the worth of a child? How could they be in a fog about something so important? They may have meant well but they were way out of line.

Love has two sides

So Jesus' love, like a coin, has two sides to it. It blends softness and sternness, and we must look at both sides to get a right understanding of it. Softness alone, with no indignation in it, would make Jesus' love weak and spineless, and give it a false tolerance. But sternness alone, with no compassion in it, would make his attitude harsh and cruel, and give it a false intolerance. Jesus' love combined both.

He had a deep concern for others that made his love warm and attractive. He went about doing good. He was constantly reaching out in kindness and helpfulness. But when he encountered hurtful, harmful things like hypocrisy, falsehood, and deceit, and found them entrenched in human hearts, his love recoiled from them, for such things blight mens' bodies and damn their souls. And his love boiled over in righteous anger.

Sinful anger

Even human love has these two sides to it, for what parents would want their little child to play with a pair of scissors, or a box of matches, or something equally dangerous? Our very love makes us angry, and we take such things away with strong words of warning. True love makes us intolerant of things that deceive and destroy because of the harm they do to others. But *our* anger is too often high-jacked for selfish uses. Even small things can provide the spark that sets it alight! Somebody bumps into us, or a motorist cuts in ahead of us, or a shop assistant fails to please us, or a member of the family contradicts us, and we immediately become indignant! Yet I know from my own heart that the giant evils of our day can leave us as calm as a windless summer morning.

A creative force

We must heed the warnings of Ephesians 4:26–27: 'In your anger do not sin: Do not let the sun go down while you are still angry, and do not give the devil a foothold.' These verses do not forbid anger, for it can be harnessed for good. It can be a creative force that gets things done. It has played a vital part in many of the reforms that stand out like bright lights on the pages of history. It certainly played its part in the life of Anthony Cooper, 7th Earl of Shaftesbury, one of the great reformers. One day, when he was a schoolboy at Harrow, he saw a pauper's funeral that impressed him deeply. A memorial tablet, reputedly close to the spot, records the incident. It says that he saw the funeral 'with shame and indignation' and that it 'helped to awaken his life-long devotion to the service of the poor and oppressed'.

The same indignation has sparked many a helpful reform. It played its part in Elizabeth Fry's prison reforms, in Robert Owen's factory reforms, and in William Wilberforce's battle against slavery. It plays its part today in the work amongst abused children and battered wives, and in other areas of cruelty and need. And God's people have been in the vanguard of such reforms, for if we know but a little of Christ's love in our hearts we shall feel a sense of outrage at some of the things that happen in our world. At the very least it will send us to prayer to enlist God's help.

Anger on a leash

But anger, like fire, can get out of control, so we must be careful. It can lapse into bad temper, and make us irritable and irascible. It can bubble away like a hot spring and have a scalding effect on others. A man took his friend to task because he could not control his temper. He tried to justify himself by saying that his temper tantrums did not last long. His friend replied, 'An earthquake does not last long but it does a great deal of damage while it lasts!'

So the apostle says, 'In your anger do not sin. Do not let the sun go down while you are still angry'. And in Greek, Paul's second word for anger is a stronger word. It suggests an anger that is being nursed and nourished. It has bitterness and vindictiveness in it, which feeds the desire for revenge. So Paul tells us not go to bed boiling away inside. He urges us to deal with our anger a day at a time, for that will keep it within bounds. If we hang on to it we shall give the devil a foothold in our lives, and he only needs a foothold to play havoc with us, for he knows how to plant thoughts and ideas in our minds that will keep our anger on the boil. He encourages it, for it can make us do foolish and hurtful things that will ruin our testimony.

So let us ask the Lord Jesus every day for *his* love, for that will guard our anger from the wrong things, and salvage it for the right things.

The apostle Paul

We see this in the life of the apostle Paul. The love that *he* showed came from this divine spring. He told the Christians at Philippi that he longed for them all 'with the affection of Christ Jesus' (Philippians 1:8). And he told the Christians at Corinth, 'For Christ's love compels us' (2 Corinthians 5:14), and the Greek word for 'compels' suggests that this love hemmed Paul in just as a narrow gorge hems in the river that flows through it. It kept him on the pathway of Christian service, constantly reaching out to others. It proved a powerful motivating force in his life, making him the man of God that he was. And because Paul's love came from this spring, he showed the same intolerance at times that Christ showed, for he had the same deep concern for others.

Paul's defence of the gospel

His letter to the Galatians shows us how intolerant he was when faced with attacks on the gospel, which spells out God's way of salvation. The Christians in Galatia had embraced it with great eagerness, and were forging ahead in the Christian life. But then false teachers got in amongst them, like wolves amongst lambs. Paul was most indignant, for what these men were teaching undermined the very foundations of the gospel. It posed a serious threat to its saving truth, and was like the holing of lifeboats on a sinking ship.

Paul says, 'I am astonished that you are so quickly deserting the one who called you by the grace of Christ and are turning to a different gospel—which is really no gospel at all. Evidently some people are throwing you into confusion and are trying to pervert the gospel of Christ' (1:6–7). Their betrayal angered Paul, but like the anger of Jesus it had grief as well as granite in it. His heart ached for these Christians in Galatia, for he could see how they were being led astray.

So Paul took his stand for the truth. He insisted that the gospel is not negotiable because the Lord himself had given it to him. No man had handed it to him. He says, 'the gospel I preached is not something that man made up. I did not receive it from any man, nor was I taught it; rather, I received it by revelation from Jesus Christ' (1:11–12). And in the first two chapters he uses extracts from his diary to prove it, for so much was at stake. So we can trace the gospel like some great river to its hidden source in the hills of God's love. It has no human origin; it comes from the heart of God. It is *his* way of rescuing us from our sins and putting us right with himself.

Love does not embrace everything

So in defending the gospel Paul does not mince his words. He says, 'But even if we or an angel from heaven should preach a gospel other than the one we preached to you, let him be eternally condemned!' (1:8). And he underlines it by repeating it: 'As we have already said, so now I say again: If anybody is preaching to you a gospel other than what you accepted, let him be eternally condemned!' (1:9). You might say, 'What intolerance! What a denial of Christian love!' But Paul writes these words in the context of love.

In chapter 5, he stresses the priority and importance of love in the Christian life. He says, 'For in Christ Jesus neither circumcision nor uncircumcision has any value. The only thing that counts is faith expressing itself through love' (v. 6). He says, 'You, my brothers, were called to be free. But do not use your freedom to indulge the sinful nature; rather, serve one another in love. The entire law is summed up in a single command: 'Love your neighbour as yourself'" (vv. 13–14). He says, 'The fruit of the Spirit is love ...' (v. 22).

Only one way of salvation

So Paul's attitude to the false teachers is in no way a denial of Christian love, for such love does not embrace everything. It reaches out to everyone with kindness and concern but it does not embrace falsehood and error that are so destructive. God's love walks hand in hand with God's truth and supports it unreservedly. It vigorously opposes any attempt to pervert the gospel of Christ, for it enshrines God's only way of salvation. He has no other way of restoring our broken relationship with himself. God saves us by grace alone, through faith alone, in Christ alone. Those three phrases summarize the gospel perfectly, and we must neither add to them nor subtract from them. Any additions or subtractions only pervert the gospel.

Some doctrines, like the doctrine of the Millennium, lie at the circumference of our Faith, and different views should not prevent us from enjoying fellowship in the Lord, or hinder us from working together. We should have no hesitation in reaching out across denominational divides. But other doctrines, like the doctrine of salvation, lie at the heart of our Faith where different views are extremely serious. There is no room for them because there is only one gospel. Jude, in his letter, refers to 'the faith that was once for all entrusted to the saints' (v. 3), and he urges us to 'contend' for it. I know we live in a multi-faith society but God's truth has not changed. We must fight hard for the purity of the gospel, for it is still the only way of salvation. Love will determine how we fight for it and will save us from arrogance and harshness, but we *must* make a stand.

Isaiah 45:22 makes it crystal clear that God alone can rescue us from our sins and reconcile us to himself. For he says, 'Turn to *me* and be saved, all you ends of the earth; for I am God and there is no other.' We get the same insistence from God's Son, the Lord Jesus Christ. He said, 'I am the way and the truth and the life. *No-one* comes to the Father *except through me*' (John 14:6). And when Peter and John stood before the Jewish Sanhedrin Peter said, 'Salvation is found in no-one else, for there is no other name under heaven given to men by which we must be saved' (Acts 4:12). Peter could not make it any clearer. The phrases 'No-one else', and 'no other name', shut us up completely to the Lord Jesus Christ. We must pin all our hopes on him for he alone can put us right with God.

We get the same truth in 1 Timothy 2:5–6. Paul says, 'There is one God and one mediator between God and men, the man Christ Jesus, who gave himself as a ransom for all men—the testimony given in its proper time.' 'One God', 'one mediator', and 'one ransom'. Again Paul could not make it any clearer. He goes on, 'And for this purpose I was appointed a herald and an apostle—I am telling the truth, I am not lying—and a teacher of the true faith to the Gentiles' (v. 7).

Peter's hypocrisy

So when it becomes necessary, Christian love, far from embracing everything, will resist those who pervert or distort the gospel. In Galatians 2:11, Paul refers to another page in his diary. He says, 'When Peter came to Antioch, I opposed him to his face, because he was clearly in the wrong.' What an explosive situation! Here were two leading apostles locking horns in open conflict, and it was all because of the gospel.

Paul tells us what happened. When Peter first arrived in Antioch, Jewish and Gentile believers worshipped and worked together quite happily. And Peter had no scruples about eating with the Gentiles; he enjoyed their fellowship in Christ. And they not only had meals together; they doubtless shared in the Lord's Supper. But then a group of men arrived from Jerusalem saying they had come from James, the leader of the church there. They claimed to have his authority, although later James denied that, Acts 15:24. And they started preaching, 'Unless you are circumcised, according to the custom taught by Moses, you cannot be saved' (Acts 15:1). That sent a shock wave through the Gentile Christians and threw them into confusion.

The fall-out proved very serious because it brought division into the church. Peter began to cut himself off from the Gentile believers. He no longer felt free to eat with them or to share in the Lord's Supper with them. Paul branded Peter's behaviour as 'hypocrisy' (Galatians 2:13), for he was not acting from conviction. He was just playing a part. The Greek word for hypocrite was used originally of an actor in the theatre who hid behind a mask, pretending to be somebody he was not. So the word came to mean any kind of pretence, and has the idea of deceitfulness in it.

Peter wanted to make a good impression on these men from Jerusalem, on those who belonged to 'the circumcision group' (v. 12), so he pretended loyalty to the Law of Moses when all the time he was acting out of fear. Maybe he was afraid for his reputation! What a clear illustration of Proverbs 29:25: 'Fear of man will prove to be a snare'. It certainly trapped Peter, and the other Jews like a lot of sheep followed his lead. They joined him behind his mask, and even Barnabas was deceived, for he too took part in the charade.

Paul confronts Peter

Paul watched with dismay as those he loved in the Lord were swept away on a tide of inconsistency. He himself stood as firm as a rock while this tide swirled around him, for his love, far from making him weak and flabby, put iron into his soul. True love makes no terms with evil whatever form it takes. When necessity demands, love drags it into the open and resists it without compromise.

Paul saw clearly what was happening and it was not a time to handle the situation with kid gloves. He had to take decisive action, for Peter's behaviour was contradicting the only gospel and leading the other Jews astray. Paul says, 'they were not acting in line with the truth of the gospel' (v. 14), so he confronted Peter publicly. And he took the teaching of this pressure group apart, for it was way off-beam.

Its disastrous effects

First of all, *it corrupted God's way of salvation*. It added works to faith, for these men from Jerusalem insisted on circumcision, which is something *we* must do. And it opens the door to a whole lot more, but Paul says to Peter, 'We ... know that a man is not justified by observing the law, but by faith in Jesus Christ' (vv. 15–16). And Peter *did* know that. He knew that we cannot work our way into God's good books by circumcision or by anything else, for his pass mark is one hundred per cent and none of us can reach that.

Romans 3 makes that crystal clear. It indicts every one of us, Jews and Gentiles, for it says, 'There is no-one righteous, not even one … There is no difference, for all have sinned and fall short of the glory of God' (vv. 10, 22).

How grateful we should be, then, for *God's* plan of salvation. He saves us through faith in the Lord Jesus Christ, and through faith alone. That slams the door on circumcision and anything else we might do. As Paul reminded Peter, 'We, too'—we Jews as well as the Gentiles—'have put our faith in Christ Jesus that we may be justified'—accepted as righteous—'by faith in Christ and not by observing the law' (Galatians 2:16). Good works provide the evidence of salvation, but they in no way contribute to it.

Secondly, what this pressure group taught *detracted from the sufficiency of Christ.* As Paul talked to Peter he kept on stressing not just 'faith' but 'faith in Christ' for as we have stressed already Jesus Christ is the only Saviour. Faith links us to him as couplings on a train link the engine to its carriages. They do not pull the carriages, for the engine alone can do that, but like faith in Christ they provide the vital link.

By insisting on circumcision these false teachers were teaching that something more was needed. They were adding something to Christ as though *he* were not able to save us. They were undermining his atoning work, and disparaging his gift of righteousness. So they were implying that Jesus is not a saving Saviour. Paul denounced such teaching for it is an affront to God. It attacks the very heart of the gospel. He says bluntly, 'If righteousness could be gained through the law, Christ died for nothing' (Galatians 2:21).

Thirdly, this insistence on circumcision *shattered the unity of the church.* Paul says that Peter 'began to draw back and separate himself from the Gentiles', and the other Jews followed suit. The fellowship they had been enjoying broke down. What a tragedy! This false teaching drove a wedge between the believing Jews and the believing Gentiles. It acted as a surgical knife cutting the Body of Christ in two. Paul *had* to denounce it for it was a violation of Christian love. He could not stand idly by and see the church at Antioch wreck itself on the rocks of falsehood and error.

The coin of love

Wherever we see this love in circulation we find it has these two sides to it, a softer side and a sterner side. We find it in the life of Christ himself. We find it in the life of the apostle Paul. And we find it in the lives of all those imbued with this same love.

It does not embrace everything. It is not credulous or naïve, for it has a discernment all its own. It champions righteousness and truth. It opposes evil and error because they bring disaster to so many people. We must read all this into Paul's exhortation, 'Follow the way of love …' (1 Corinthians 14:1).

Watch your words

We trade in words every day. They pour into our world like a flood, in all sorts of ways, and we all add our own little stream. And we can toss words about thoughtlessly and carelessly as though they had no more effect than table tennis balls, but they can be as lethal as grenades. Words matter. Petersen brings this out in his paraphrase of James 3:5: 'A word out of your mouth may seem of no account, but it can accomplish nearly anything—or destroy it!' So we must watch our words, for they can have a profound effect on our relationships.

Words can do so much good. They can bring two people very close together. They can bring warmth, sympathy, and understanding into the church. They can please, help, and inspire. They can enrich and encourage in a thousand different ways. They can put the discouraged back on their feet, and lift their spirits on the darkest day. They can refresh the weary, like water from a fountain. Proverbs 10:11 makes that very point: 'The mouth of the righteous is a fountain of life'.

But words can also do a great deal of harm. They can offend, hinder, and inflame. They can drive two people apart. They can stir up strife, conflict, and violence. They can wreck a church, and tear it apart. They can shatter confidence, bring discouragement, and plunge into despair. They can pour over us like boiling water, scalding and scarring. They can defile, deprave, and destroy. They can ruin relationships, and put them beyond repair. So we *must* watch our words, or we could hurt and wound those around us.

So much evil flows into our world through the tongue, and we can still have trouble with it after God saves us. James develops this theme in his letter. In his very practical way, and with many arresting illustrations, he brings faith into the arena of life. And in chapter 3, he has some hard-hitting things to say about the tongue. To read this chapter is like walking through an art gallery! With one picture after another James lights up the truth, exploding it in our hearts and minds like a batch of fireworks.

Show me your tongue

James makes the use of the tongue a test of spiritual maturity. In v.2 he says,

'We all stumble in many ways. If anyone is never at fault in what he says, he is a perfect man, able to keep his whole body in check.' Like a doctor checking on our health, James says, 'Show me your tongue!' For if we can control our tongue, and use it wisely and well, we are really making progress in the Christian life. And what a difference it makes in our relationships.

Our words provide windows into our hearts, as Jesus made clear to the Pharisees. In Matthew 12:34, he says, 'Out of the overflow of the heart the mouth speaks.' When we are full of something, the mouth takes the overflow. If envy, or bitterness, or hatred fills our hearts, our words will give us away, for we shall overflow at the mouth. If love, kindness, and compassion fill our hearts, we shall still overflow at the mouth, but how differently! Our words will spill out in help, support, and encouragement.

Because our words are so revealing, they may be used against us on the Day of Judgement. In Matthew 12, Jesus says, 'The good man brings good things out of the good stored up in him, and the evil man brings evil things out of the evil stored up in him. But I tell you that men will have to give account on the Day of Judgment for every careless word they have spoken. For by your words you will be acquitted, and by your words you will be condemned' (vv. 35–37).

Note that Jesus says 'every *careless* word' because our carefully chosen words, like windows of frosted glass, may reveal very little. Our most revealing words are unpremeditated. We have no time, or we see no need, to dress them up. We may speak when we are off guard, or in the heat of the moment, and if our hearts are not right, the words will flow from our tongue like water from a dirty spring. How that presses home our need of a Saviour! For God records everything, even our careless words, and they will be called as evidence for the prosecution on the great Day of Judgement. God only forgets what he has forgiven.

The tongue's influence

James describes the tongue as 'a small part of the body' (v. 5), but it has an influence far beyond its size. James illustrates this from the 'bit' in v. 3, and the 'rudder' in v. 4. He says, 'When we put bits into the mouths of horses to make them obey us, we can turn the whole animal. Or take ships as an example. Although they are so large and are driven by strong winds, they are steered by a very small rudder wherever the pilot wants to go.' Just as the 'bit' and the 'rudder' for all their smallness, determine the direction of the 'horse' and the 'ship', so the tongue can change the direction of peoples' lives.

Preaching the truth

The tongue, yielded to the Lord, can pour out God's truth so powerfully that even hardened sinners are saved, and their lives transformed. I have seen it happen. The preacher's words may seem so weak, but the Holy Spirit can give them such sharpness and penetration that they can pierce people's defences and win them for Christ. And the tongue's influence can live on long after it falls silent.

When my twin brother and I were about fourteen years old, a group a young people shared the gospel with us. I can see them now, so keen, so eager! We were standing on a street corner, and they told us that we needed to be saved. They told us how Jesus Christ could give us peace with God, but we had no time for such a message, for we were steeped in self-righteousness. We gave those young people a hard time, and we must have discouraged them, but they sowed the truth of God's Word in our hearts that night. It was some years later before it began to germinate, but when it did we saw our need, and we put our faith in Jesus Christ the only Saviour.

That happens to so many people, so we must never judge by appearances. And no preacher should get discouraged if he sees few, if any, immediate results from his preaching. The seed of God's Word can lie dormant for years then, suddenly, be brought to life by the Holy Spirit.

Spreading encouragement

The tongue has a far greater influence than many of us realize. We can use it to encourage, but so few of us do. We find it easier to grumble or complain! In all four churches I pastored, I had members who encouraged me, and I thank God for them, but they were in the minority. I want to make a plea for the ministry of encouragement. Such a ministry is open to all of us, it is so much needed, and it can do so much good.

Just a few timely words can brighten up another's day like a shaft of sunlight on a dark day. I know that from experience. I have had a letter, a card, or a phone call at just the right time, and it has acted like a 'rudder' guiding me into the calm of the Saviour's peace. I have pressed on with a new awareness of God, and a new spring in my step.

What a lovely name the apostles gave Joseph, the Levite from Cyprus. He was a great encouragement to them, and they saw him encouraging others in so many ways. Words of encouragement dripped from his tongue like honey. So they called him Barnabas, that means 'Son of Encouragement' (Acts 4:36), and he certainly lived up to his name.

He encouraged the church by his generous giving, for it reflected his devotion to Christ. When the church in Jerusalem shunned the newly converted Saul of Tarsus because of suspicion and unbelief, Barnabas pleaded for his acceptance, and he *was* accepted. For according to Acts 9:28: 'Saul stayed with them and moved about freely in Jerusalem, speaking boldly in the name of the Lord.' Barnabas was contagiously encouraging wherever he went.

In 1 Thessalonians 4, Paul writes to believers grappling with grief, a grief made worse because they thought their loved ones would miss all the glory of the Lord's return. Paul puts them right on that in v.16. He says, 'The dead in Christ will rise first.' Far from missing out they will be given priority. They will have the front seats. What an encouragement! But Paul urges mutual encouragement, for in v. 18, he says, 'Therefore encourage *each other* with these words.' These are the things we should talk about when bereavement comes.

We live in a troubled, hurting world, and so many people need to be encouraged. So let the honey of encouragement drop on others from your tongue. Be a Barnabas!

Inflammatory words

Use your tongue to help others, not destroy them, for as James 3 tells us, words can be as destructive as fire. In v. 5, he says, 'Consider what a great forest is set on fire by a small spark.' Many a blaze has started that way. A dropped match or a cigarette butt could be the culprit. It begins to smoulder and then it bursts into a flame that spreads for miles.

When I was in Chicago recently, I thought about the famous fire there in

1871. It left 100,000 people homeless, destroyed 17,500 buildings, and killed 300 people. And it cost thousands of dollars. And it all began with a tiny flame. A woman was milking her cow, and she had a little oil lamp. The cow kicked it over and the flame kindled a wisp of hay, and another wisp, and another wisp, until the whole building was ablaze. Soon the next building caught fire, and the next, and the next, until whole streets had succumbed to the flames.

In v. 6, James says, 'The tongue also is a fire', and again we see that it has an influence far beyond its size. Our words can start fires. Just a few hot, burning words can start a blaze that may prove difficult to put out. Oh what damage the tongue can do! Like fire it can leave a trail of destruction.

We find this same picture of the tongue in 'The Book of Proverbs', which has the same down to earth approach to life as James. It says, 'A scoundrel plots evil, and his speech is like a scorching fire' (16:27). In 26:20–21, it says, 'Without wood a fire goes out; without gossip a quarrel dies down. As charcoal to embers and as wood to fire, so is a quarrelsome man for kindling strife.'

Beware of gossip, for it can be most inflammatory. It can stoke up a fire already started. Gossip has been described as confessing other peoples' sins, and we have enough sins of our own to confess! And the gossip may not be true. If we have no opportunity to check it out, we should not pass it on.

One writer says, 'If all men were dumb, what a portion of the crimes of the world would soon cease! If all men would speak only that which ought to be spoken, what a change would come over the face of human affairs.' How true!

Fire from hell

What a terrible indictment of the tongue James gives us in v. 6. He describes it as 'a world of evil among the parts of the body'. For it can commit every sin in the book. It can break every one of the Ten Commandments, in spirit if not in letter. And how many sins the tongue can aggravate!

James says, 'It corrupts the whole person'. Like a rotten apple in a basket of good apples, our words will affect other areas of our lives. And they do have an effect. We can talk ourselves into discouragement and even despair.

And our words act like a boomerang on our character. If we keep using censorious words, or unkind words, or unpleasant words, we shall become increasingly censorious, or increasingly unkind, or increasingly unpleasant. For such words defile us just as fire defiles with its smoke. And they help to mould the kind of people we are.

James says, 'The tongue ... sets the whole course of his life on fire' (v. 6). It can do its evil work at any time in our lives. As John Calvin puts it, 'The vice of the tongue ... is as active and potent for evil in old age as ever it was in the days of our youth.' How important then that we watch our words, and heed the warning light that flashes from Ecclesiastes 5:6: 'Do not let your mouth lead you into sin.'

'The tongue ... is a fire', says James, and he traces this fire to its source. He says it is 'set on fire by hell'. So Satan has a hand in all this. If he gets control of the tongue he can work havoc with it. Matthew Poole, the Puritan commentator, talks about his 'bellows of temptation'. He says, 'The tongue being the fire, the devil, by the bellows of temptation, inflames it yet more and more and thereby kindles the fire of all mischief in the world.'

The whole of evil, in the whole of man, for the whole of life. What an indictment! And how skilfully James illustrates the destructive power of the tongue.

Poisonous words

In v. 8, James turns from 'fire' to 'poison'. He says the tongue 'is a restless evil, full of deadly poison'. This echoes what David says about evil men in Psalm 140:3: 'They make their tongues as sharp as a serpent's; the poison of vipers is on their lips.' What an apt picture, for that is exactly where a viper conceals its poison, in a little bag at the root of the lips. When it bites, it injects its venom into its victim. And poison, like fire, destroys. Words can spoil a home, wreck a marriage, ruin a church, and divide a community. They can blacken a reputation, foul a mind, and sour an atmosphere.

We can start a fire accidentally, but we distil poison deliberately. It is not like fire, for it works secretly and slowly and then kills. It does not need to be taken in large doses either; just a few drops will suffice. And the tongue does not need to make long speeches; the mischief can be done with just a few words. The tongue can inject real venom into a situation.

George Duncan, who had a worldwide convention ministry, never touched alcohol as a matter of principle. But one day, a member of his congregation invited him and his wife out to lunch at a certain hotel, and before they went into lunch he asked them if they would like something to drink. They said, 'Yes, thank you very much.' And they asked for Schloer, which is pure apple juice, and very refreshing. But within twenty-four hours, word reached him that a report was going round that George Duncan had been seen in the lounge of this hotel, drinking beer! Why should such a report be circulated?

Oh what poison the tongue can distil! It can happen anywhere and the poison can spread, in small ways if not in big ways. As the child's rhyme puts it, 'I lost a very little word, only the other day; It was a very naughty word I had not meant to say. But, then, it was not really lost—when from my lips it flew, my little brother picked it up, and now he says it too!'

In Psalm 141:3, David prays, 'Set a guard over my mouth, O Lord; keep watch over the door of my lips.' Let us make that our prayer, that when the door of our lips opens nothing but good might come out.

Refreshing words

For the tongue can help others so much. It can enrich relationships in home and church in so many ways. Think of the difference the words 'I love you' can make in a marriage. The tongue can distil peace as well as poison. It can refresh as well as revile. Proverbs 10:11 describes the mouth as a fountain. It says, 'The mouth of the righteous is a fountain of life', and other verses in Proverbs use the same picture. 13:14 says, 'The teaching of the wise is a fountain of life, turning a man from the snares of death.' 18:4 says, 'The words of a man's mouth are deep waters, but the fountain of wisdom is a bubbling brook.' Just as a fountain can provide cool, refreshing water, so the tongue can refresh a weary heart. Just a few words can rescue a man or a woman from discouragement, and put a new perspective on things. The tongue can be so helpful.

Nourishing words

The tongue can make food as well as fire. It can nourish as well as destroy.

Proverbs 10:21 says, 'The lips of the righteous nourish many'. Proverbs 15:4 says, 'The tongue that brings healing is a tree of life'. Just as a tree can provide food, so the tongue can feed the mind, and nourish the soul. It can strengthen the weak, and point them to the resources in Christ that can turn defeat into victory.

Paul has a searching word about this in Ephesians 4. In v. 29, he deals with the tongue in relationships and he says, 'Do not let any unwholesome talk come out of your mouths, but only what is helpful for building others up according to their needs, that it may benefit those who listen.'

The tongue's inconsistency

James, like Proverbs, uses the pictures of the 'spring' and the 'tree', but he uses them in a different way. He uses them to condemn our inconsistency. In (3:9–11) he says, 'With the tongue we praise our Lord and Father, and with it we curse men, who have been made in God's likeness. Out of the same mouth come praise and cursing. My brothers, *this should not be*. Can both fresh water and salt water flow from the same spring? My brothers, can a fig-tree bear olives, or a grapevine bear figs? Neither can a salt spring produce fresh water.' What a stream of praise can flow from the tongue! If it comes from the heart, how it enriches our worship, and glorifies God. In Psalm 51:15, David prays, 'O Lord, open my lips, and my mouth will declare your praise.' He wanted to be a true worshipper. In Psalm 63:3, he prays, 'Because your love is better than life, my lips will glorify you.' We have so much to praise God for.

But the tongue can be so inconsistent. John Blanchard recalls what a friend once told him, that one of the most challenging sermons he had ever heard was called 'Ten Minutes after the Benediction'. It spoke of those 'who moved in moments from the gloria to gossip, from creed to criticism, from worshipping God to wounding men'. What inconsistency!

James says, 'My brothers, this should not be', and he demonstrates this from nature. The Middle East has its natural springs even today. Fresh water gushes from some, and salt water from others, but none pour out both. And we would never expect to pick olives from fig trees, or figs from grapevines. That would be impossible, so even the order of nature rebukes us for our inconsistency.

Taming the tongue

What can we do about it? In vv. 7–8, James says, 'All kinds of animals, birds, reptiles and creatures of the sea are being tamed and have been tamed by man, but no man can tame the tongue.' For the problem goes deeper. Jesus made that clear when he said, 'Out of the overflow of the heart the mouth speaks.'

A Christian got angry and said something very unkind. It embarrassed him, so he said to his friend, 'I don't know why I said that. It really isn't in me!' His friend said to him, 'It had to be in you or it couldn't have come out of you!' That takes us to the core of the problem. An unruly tongue stems from an undisciplined heart.

The Holy Spirit

The healing work must be done in the heart, where the Saviour indwells his people by his Spirit. He can tame the tongue by bringing the heart under his control. I have seen him do it. He can take a filthy tongue and clean it up. He can take a blaspheming tongue and use it to bless God. He can take a backbiting, scandal-mongering tongue, and transform it by his love. He can take a complaining tongue and make it flow with thanksgiving. He can take a lying tongue and make it an instrument for truth.

How significant that when the Holy Spirit came at Pentecost the disciples 'saw what seemed to be *tongues* of fire that separated and came to rest on each of them' (Acts 2:3). James writes about the fire that comes from hell, but this fire came from heaven. And what a different effect it had on the tongue! 'All of them were filled with the Holy Spirit and began to speak in other tongues as the Spirit enabled them' (Acts 2:4). And the jostling crowd, amazed and perplexed said, 'We hear them declaring the wonders of God in our own tongues!' (v. 11).

In Ephesians 5:1,8 Paul says, 'Be filled with the Spirit', and he forges the same link with the tongue. For in vv. 19–20, he says, 'Speak to one another with psalms, hymns and spiritual songs. Sing and make music in your heart to the Lord, always giving thanks to God the Father for everything, in the name of our Lord Jesus Christ.' We may not speak in other tongues, but if the Lord Jesus controls us by his Spirit we shall certainly use our own tongue to worship God and to enrich others. Our words will strengthen and encourage, heal and inspire, and everybody around us will benefit.

Let us seek day by day, then, to be filled with the Spirit, for if he controls our hearts he will tame our tongues. Psalm 19:14 would be an apt prayer for all of us to pray: 'May the words of my mouth and the meditation of my heart be pleasing in your sight, O Lord, my Rock and my Redeemer.'

Some home truths

Words certainly play a vital part in our relationships, especially in the home. For there, more than most places, our tongue can run away with us. We can say really hurtful things that we afterwards regret, but once said things cannot be unsaid. And words can wound with all the sharpness of a knife, and such wounds can take time to heal. So we *must* watch our words, for just a handful of them can destroy a relationship.

But we must also furnish words with deeds, for words alone can be as empty as a deserted house. James himself, who deals so searchingly with our use of the tongue, alerts us to the danger of mere words. He gives us a very clear example. He says, 'Suppose a brother or sister is without clothes and daily food. If one of you says to him, "Go, I wish you well; keep warm and well fed", but does nothing about his physical needs, what good is it?' (2:15–16). Words alone will not warm his back or fill his stomach!

The apostle John sounds the same warning. In a passage about love he says, 'Dear children, let us not love with words or tongue but with actions and in truth' (1 John 3:18). How careful we must be about this substitution! We can slide into it so easily because words are cheap but deeds can be costly. Kind words cost nothing, but they can make us feel good even if we do not follow them up. And if we do take them further it could make big demands on us, so we do nothing. I know that from my own experience, for as a preacher, I trade in words and I *could* be content with words alone. But I want so much to practise what I preach, for love gets hold of our hands as well as our voice. It shows itself in what we do as well as in what we say. And actions speak louder! They give substance to our words, and rescue us from hypocrisy.

True love

True love combines right words with good deeds, and we need this love in *all* our relationships, but especially in the home. We need it amidst all the ups and downs of family life, for the home can be a hard place at times to be a Christian. We are seen at all hours of the day and night, so like goods in a shop window we are always on display. And we are not always at our best!

Elsewhere, under the eyes of others, we tend to keep ourselves under control, but away from the glare of public life we can let our guard down. We may be tired and frustrated, and if we have a short fuse we do not need much provocation to become angry and impatient. If the day has not gone well we can take it out on one another. Indeed we can make one another's lives a misery! Relationships can break down, and broken relationships too often lead to broken marriages with all the hurt and trauma that they bring.

God's pattern

We need help, and we can find it in God's Word, where he gives us a clear pattern for family life. Marriages break down and children are left frightened and insecure because we ignore this pattern. The apostle Peter spells it out for us in 1 Peter 3, and the first thing we note is that he roots it *in people not things*. He says, 'Wives …' (v. 1), and 'Husbands …' (v. 7). He says nothing about possessions that tend to play such a big part in our lives.

One day the Lord Jesus said, 'Watch out! Be on your guard against all kinds of greed; a man's life does not consist in the abundance of his possessions' (Luke 12:15). How we need to shout this from the rooftops today! And how we should heed it in our homes, for the secret of a happy home does not lie in possessions.

We must keep that in mind if we visit 'The Ideal Homes Exhibition' at Earl's Court in London, or at the King's Hall in Belfast. It puts all sorts of things on display from furniture to kitchen equipment, as though *that* were the key to an ideal home! We must not be misled or we shall be so busy putting our house right that we never build a home. And our children *need* a home where they feel comfortable, where they feel loved and wanted. It will keep them from going astray and getting into trouble.

Husbands and wives

In 1 Peter 3, then, Peter roots God's pattern for the home in people, not things. And he roots it secondly *in the relationship between husbands and wives*. He bases everything on that, for it lies at the foundation of a happy home. In Ephesians 5, the apostle Paul does the same. He says, 'Wives, submit to your husbands as to the Lord' (v. 22). And he says, 'Husbands, love your wives, just as Christ loved the church' (v. 25). Only then does he deal with the relationship between parents and children.

This ties in with a quotation I have from a child psychologist whose name I do not remember. He said, 'It is more important for parents to love each other than for parents to love their children.' How true! A loving relationship between a husband and wife that embraces their children will give them a far greater feeling of security than anything either parent can do for them. But if they grow up amidst rows and arguments that boil over because their parents do not get on with each other, it will have the opposite effect on them. It could scar them for life.

How important then that parents should guard their relationship! We should make time for one another, and not take one another for granted. We should learn to value one another, and to observe the common courtesies of life, especially 'Please' and 'Thank you', for that makes such a difference. And so do those three little words, 'I love you'. They can bring much welcome reassurance. And the Lord Jesus can help us, as we share our lives day by day with him he can keep us sweet inside.

Rights and responsibilties

Thirdly, Peter roots God's pattern for family life *in responsibilities not rights*. How refreshing, for we hear so much about rights today. Perhaps if more people shouldered their responsibilities we would hear far less about rights! In 1 Peter 3, the apostle says nothing about rights; he deals only with responsibilities. He redresses the balance that has been lost today. This does not make his teaching very popular, but an insistence on rights will soon wreck a marriage, for it is not that kind of relationship. Peter says to both husbands and wives, 'You have responsibilities!'

But he says so much more to wives than he does to husbands because they would have the greater problems. If a husband became a Christian he would take his wife to church with him automatically. There would be no discussion about it. But if a wife became a Christian and her husband did not, she could find herself in a difficult position. Women did not enjoy the freedom they do today, so a Christian wife had to be very careful how she behaved. She needed help, so Peter takes time over it. He tells her how to win her unsaved husband for Christ.

Wives are no longer put in such a position, but even today the conversion of one partner can put a marriage under strain. I knew a couple that got married before either of them knew the Saviour. Like many other couples they had a church wedding and made their vows before God, but they did not know him. Then one day the husband was converted. He had a life-changing encounter with the Lord Jesus Christ, and it showed. But his wife was none too pleased, and that brought tensions into the home that had not been there before. She resented what had happened to him. She said that he was no longer the man she married, and she was right! He loved to read his Bible, but that was like a red rag to a bull! Then one day the wife herself was converted, and that transformed the whole situation.

Character

Fourthly, Peter roots God's pattern for marriage *in our character*. He tells wives to be submissive, pure, reverent, and attractive. He talks about their 'inner self', and 'the unfading beauty of a gentle and quiet spirit' (v. 4). These are all qualities of character. Peter tells husbands to be considerate, respectful, and prayerful (v. 7). Again, these are all qualities of character. So Peter majors on what we are, rather than on what we do. For that is the spring from which our actions flow, and what a lovely spring it is! But we must examine it carefully to appreciate that.

The responsibilities of wives

Peter begins with wives, and he urges *submission*. His first word to them is, 'be submissive to your husbands' (v. 1), and that raises our hackles straightaway, for it cuts right across our natural tendencies. It seems so out of step to talk about submission when everybody is talking about equality. It seems a cringing, crawling kind of word, and that makes it very unpopular in this fight-back generation.

Charles Swindoll in his book *Hope Again* says, 'I'm convinced in my heart that if we were good students of submission we would get along a lot better in life. But I am also convinced that it is the one thing, more than any other, that works against our very natures, which argue, 'I don't want to submit. I don't want to give in. I won't let him have his way in this'. And we live abrasively'.

But submission clearly has an important place in God's plan for harmonious relationships, for Peter has already used the word twice in chapter 2. If we are God's people we must keep the word 'submission' very securely in our vocabulary for God has not cut it out of his. He certainly insists on it in his pattern for marriage.

In Ephesians 5 Paul joins hands with Peter on this. He says, 'Wives, submit to your husbands as to the Lord', v. 22. Paul, like Peter, addresses wives who are Christians, so he brings the Lord into it, for we have our relationship with him to consider. And this is something that *he* wants, so it cannot be the bad thing it is often made out to be. It gets a bad press because we misunderstand it.

The word 'submit' translates a Greek military term that means 'to fall in rank under the authority of another ... to subject oneself for the purpose of obeying or pleasing another'. Imagine an army in which there is no submission! It would disintegrate. But the word does not suggest inferiority. It implies that some must lead and others must follow. We cannot all be leaders!

God has given the leadership in marriage to the husband, so girls choosing a husband should ask themselves, 'Is this a man I could look up to? Could I accept his leadership? Do I find his lead helpful? Would I be happy to submit to him?' These questions are important, and the answers could provide just the guidance you need. It is not enough that you are both Christians. Face these questions honestly, and if you cannot answer, 'Yes', to them, do not marry him, for you would be flying in the face of God's Word.

Deeds not words

You might say, 'My husband is not a Christian. Do I still have to submit to him? Do I still have to accept his leadership?' Peter says, 'Yes!' He says if you submit to him you may well see him won for Christ. And he insists on deeds not words. He says that words must take a back seat. He says, 'Wives ... be submissive to your husbands so that, if any of them do not believe the word, they may be won over *without words* by the behaviour of their wives ...' (v. 1). So do not become over-anxious and start preaching at your husband. Do not try and nag him into the kingdom, for that will do more harm than good.

At the heart of this submission lies submission to God. If he has saved you and not your husband he knows your situation, so put it unreservedly into his hands. Put your husband at the top of your prayer list, and persevere in prayer for him. Pray with faith and expectancy, and ask God to save him not just for your comfort, although it would make such a difference, but for his glory.

I asked a woman once why she was praying for her unsaved husband. She gave me several reasons, but she said nothing about the glory of God. I pointed this out to her and urged her to lift her sights in prayer, and to pray for God's glory in her husband's conversion. She did, and one day her husband began to come to church. He got more and more interested until at last he opened his heart to the Saviour. To seek something for God's glory rescues our praying from selfishness. So check your motive in praying for your husband and if necessary, lift your sights. You cannot change your husband but God can, so trust *him* to work that life-changing miracle. And pray that he will get the glory.

And put God first in your own life. Seek his help to be the kind of wife that Peter describes here, for you will certainly need his help. God's Word sets a high standard. Spend time with your husband. Do not neglect him by going to too many meetings. Show him your love in the little things as well as in the bigger things of life.

Submission—but not too far

But we must not take this submission too far. It does not exclude discussion and disagreement, for in every marriage there must be give and take. And the Bible nowhere insists that a wife should stay in a situation that would threaten her health or endanger her life, or the lives of her children. That would be pushing submission to extremes, and making it mean what it does not. Submission has been described as 'a voluntary unselfishness', which makes it an attitude of mind. It means that when you got married you accepted your husband's leadership, so follow his lead unless he tries to lead you astray.

Be pure

The second thing that Peter urges on wives is *purity*. He says, 'your husbands' who 'do not believe the word … may be won over … when they see the purity … of your lives' (vv. 1–2). This purity has its roots in loyalty, the kind of loyalty that a couple promise each other on their wedding day. I have said to many a bridegroom as he has stood next to his bride, 'Will you love her, comfort her, honour and keep her, in sickness and in health, and be faithful to her for the rest of your life?' And he has promised his loyalty with the words, 'I will'. And I have said the same thing to the bride who has made the same promise of loyalty. To make it more personal, I have got them to turn to each other and to look at each other as they make their promises.

Such loyalty must be carefully guarded, for passing time and changing circumstances makes it vulnerable. It could well come under attack as both husband and wife meet new people. For new relationships can bring alluring temptations to unfaithfulness. Many a wife has strayed in such circumstances—and many a husband too!

But God meant marriage to be an exclusive and enduring relationship, for at the very first wedding in Genesis 2, he said, 'A man will leave his father and mother and be united to his wife, and they will become one flesh' (Genesis 2:24). What a close relationship that suggests, for the Hebrew word for 'united' conveys the thought of sticking together. It pictures a husband and wife clinging to each other as though they would never let each other go. What a great picture of marriage! It leaves no room for disloyalty, for no third party could squeeze into such a relationship.

Be respectful

The third thing that Peter urges on wives is *respect*. He twins 'purity' with 'reverence' (v. 2), which has the idea of respect in it. It encourages a right attitude to your husband when you find out what he is really like. And you *will* discover that! For you will see your husband at his worst as well as at his best. You will know him better than anyone else knows him, for you will see all his faults and weaknesses. But throughout your relationship you must go on looking up to him. If you find that difficult, look beyond your husband to the Lord and seek his help. For how essential this respect is! No marriage will survive without it.

Be attractive

With his careful choice of the words 'submissive', 'purity', and 'reverence',

Peter builds up a great picture of the Christian wife. And what desirable qualities he encourages! We see just *how* desirable if we compare them with their opposites—aggressive, flirtatious, and contemptuous. What an unpleasant wife *they* conjure up! No Christian woman would want to be that kind of wife.

So the final thing that Peter urges on wives is *attractiveness*, and he probes much deeper than outward appearance. He says, 'Your beauty should not come from outward adornment, such as braided hair and the wearing of gold jewellery and fine clothes. Instead, it should be that of your inner self, the unfading beauty of a gentle and quiet spirit, which is of great worth in God's sight' (vv. 3–4).

Every Christian wife should be concerned about her beauty, for it is no mark of spirituality to look dowdy! But real beauty does not come from externals. It does not depend on clothes, or jewellery, or hair-dos. Peter does not forbid these things, for he includes clothes, but the beauty that lasts goes a lot deeper than that. It is not something put on from the outside; it comes from within. It is like the beauty of a butterfly wrapped up in a chrysalis. It forms within and blossoms out.

Peter says to every Christian wife, 'Your beauty ... should be that of your inner self', so it is beauty of character. He describes it as 'the unfading beauty of a gentle and quiet spirit'. But how does such a beauty develop? It comes from a life open to God, a life shared with the Lord Jesus Christ and enriched daily by his grace. And God values it immensely. Every wife should be keen to possess such beauty, for it will make her husband more and more proud of her as the years go by.

Peter wants to put it into a picture, so he reaches back to 'the holy women of the past' (v. 5): for that is the way *they* made themselves beautiful. He says, 'They were submissive to their own husbands', and he picks out Abraham's wife, Sarah, as a notable example. She called her husband 'her master' (v. 6), and that speaks volumes. It shows what great respect she had for him, and her willingness to follow his lead. So her beauty came from within.

Husbands, too, have responsibilities

Peter says, 'Husbands, in the same way be considerate as you live with your wives, and treat them with respect as the weaker partner and as heirs with you of the gracious gift of life, so that nothing will hinder your prayers' (v. 7). Peter may compress what he has to say to husbands into a single verse, but if we all showed our wives the concern and courtesy that Peter urges on us here, many a home would be transformed.

Be considerate

Peter urges husbands, first of all, *to be considerate*. He has already urged that on wives so now he says, 'Husbands, in the same way be considerate'. That demands a very practical knowledge that does not come naturally or automatically. A husband must get to know his wife, her moods, hopes, and fears. That means he must spend time with her that he might cultivate their relationship as carefully as a gardener cultivates a rare flower. I have discovered the importance of this in my own life. For years now I have made a special effort to carve out quality time with my wife, and reaped the dividends of it.

Warren Wiersbe in his book *Be Hopeful* says that, 'One survey revealed that the average husband and wife had thirty-seven minutes a week together in actual communication!' He says, 'Is it any wonder that marriages fall apart after the children grow up and leave home? The husband and wife are left alone—to live with strangers!' How sad!

Peter says, 'be considerate as you live with your wives', and the word 'live' means much more than sharing the same address, or living in the same house. It takes in the sexual side of marriage, and includes caring for your wife and providing for her. We must pack all this into the consideration that Peter encourages.

Be respectful

Peter urges husbands, secondly, *to be respectful*. He says, 'be considerate as you live with your wives, and treat them with respect'. When a boy courts a girl he can be very kind and courteous, and when they get engaged he can be even more thoughtful. But when a couple get married that so often changes, for a husband can begin to take his wife for granted. He no longer honours her, as he should. How practical the Bible is! How it penetrates into the hidden places of our lives!

What can we do to halt the slide? We should resolve never to treat our wives with any less respect than we would treat any other woman. I have taught this in many a Marriage Counselling Class, for I have found it to be a helpful guiding principle. It lifts our sights straightaway, and rebukes our lowered standards. It encourages courtesy, which is love in the small things. It keeps chivalry alive, and makes for happiness in any home.

The weaker partner

Peter gives us two reasons why we should treat our wives with respect. The first reason is *physical*. He says, 'treat them with respect as the weaker partner'. People who quibble with that are going against reality. If a number of men had a tug of war with the same number of women, the men would soon pull the women over the line! There is no doubt that most husbands are physically stronger than their wives. They need our protection, and that makes a strong argument for chivalry.

It may be dead today but if we adopted Warren Wiersbe's suggestion, it would soon be resurrected. He says, 'Every husband must be a 'knight in shining armour' who treats his wife like a princess.' What a delightful picture! It ties in with a bit of symbolism that I always observed after a wedding service. I made sure that when a couple came out of the church the bride always walked on the bridegroom's left. That would leave his right arm free to protect her, and pictured the days when the right arm would have been the sword arm. What days of chivalry they were!

God's heirs

The second reason that Peter gives for showing our wives respect is *spiritual*. He says, 'treat them with respect … as heirs with you of the gracious gift of life'. I like Petersen's paraphrase: 'But in the new life of God's grace, you're equals.' Our wives may be physically weaker than us, but they are not inferior. As God's children, we belong to the same family, we have the same Saviour, we depend on the same grace, and we enjoy the same gift of eternal life.

And everything we share in Christ is an argument for treating our wives with courtesy and concern. For we share so much. We are not only God's children, we are God's heirs, and we look forward to the same spiritual inheritance. We travel the same path, and pursue the same goal. God has prepared a fabulous future for us that defies description. It takes a word like 'glory' with its suggestions of splendour, light, and beauty, to convey something of its magnificence.

Be prayerful

Peter urges husbands, finally, *to be prayerful*. He pegs all these things into our prayer life—'so that nothing will hinder your prayers'. We cannot stress too much the importance of prayer, for it keeps our lives open to God. It taps heaven's resources for earth's needs. It brings God's reinforcements marching to our aid. But we cannot divorce our prayer life from our home life.

If we fail to treat our wives with the love and care that Peter urges on us here, we shall find that God has gone deaf. Failure at home will affect the efficacy of our prayers. However many trucks we send to heaven they will all come back empty. For our relationship with God depends very much on our relationships with others.

Back to God's pattern

God's pattern for marriage is like the maker's instructions that come with most things we buy. We should study it carefully and follow it step by step. It combines both words and deeds, but we have seen that actions speak louder. And it prompts us all to examine ourselves, for if we ignore this pattern it is hardly surprising that so many things go wrong. Marriages break up and children are left frightened and insecure because we insist on going our own way. Let us get back to God's pattern for, as our Maker, he knows best.

Love's pathway

Our relationships with one another have a profound effect on our relationship with God. For it grieves *him*, as it would grieve any loving father, to see his children at loggerheads. And it hinders his work, ties his hands, and robs us of his power, both in the church and in our own lives.

How significant that the only petition in the Family Prayer that Jesus commented on was the petition to do with relationships: 'Forgive us our debts, as we also have forgiven our debtors', Matthew 6:12. At the end of the prayer Jesus said, 'For if you forgive men when they sin against you, your heavenly Father will also forgive you. But if you do not forgive men their sins, your Father will not forgive your sins', vv. 14–15. How that underscores the importance of right relationships amongst God's children!

Paul deals extensively with relationships in Ephesians 4–5, and at the very heart of that passage he says, 'And do not grieve the Holy Spirit of God, with whom you were sealed for the day of redemption', 4:30. Mark the word 'And' for it anchors this verse very securely to its context. Paul has been writing about lying, anger, stealing, and unwholesome talk, all of which involve others, and then he says, 'Do not forget the Holy Spirit in all this!' And we *can* forget him because he is so self-effacing.

Sometimes at night, an important building stands illuminated. Floodlights have been strategically placed, not that they might be seen, but that the building might be seen! The Holy Spirit has that kind of ministry. He does not draw attention to himself; he is always drawing attention to the Lord Jesus. He wants *him* to be seen. Jesus told his disciples, 'He will testify about me' (John 15:26). For that reason we can easily forget him, for the Holy Spirit keeps the spotlight on Christ. He himself stays in the background, but how much we need him! We can accomplish nothing without him.

Zechariah 4:6 comes echoing across the centuries: '"Not by might nor by power, but by my Spirit," says the Lord Almighty.' How that underscores our dependence on him! Pentecost demonstrates that. In Acts 1, the church is like a spacecraft on the ground, its engines silent. But in Acts 2, the Holy Spirit comes, the church's engines burst into life, and we have lift-off! The church begins its orbit around the world—'Jerusalem ... Judea and Samaria ... and ... the ends of the earth' (Acts 1:8). God's people, in partnership with the Spirit, become compelling witnesses to a crucified, risen, victorious Saviour. On the Day of Pentecost alone, about 3,000 people responded to the gospel! What victories of grace and power!

No wonder Paul wrote, 'And do not grieve the Holy Spirit of God, with whom you were sealed for the day of redemption' (Ephesians 4:30). But see how he continues—he moves right on into the realm of relationships. He says, 'Get rid of all bitterness, rage and anger, brawling and slander, along with every form of malice' (v. 31). Then he turns the coin over, from the things that grieve the Spirit to the things that please him. He says, 'Be kind and compassionate to one another, forgiving each other, just as in Christ God forgave you' (v. 32).

Guard that relationship

From the moment God saves us we begin a personal relationship with the Holy Spirit, and we *must* guard that relationship, for he comes to set up God's kingdom in our hearts. He comes as Jesus' representative—his 'Other Self'—to make him real to us, and to bring us increasingly under his rule. He comes as God's seal upon our lives, to give us assurance. He comes to help us in the pursuit of holiness, which we find so hard. Our own unaided efforts have failure written all over them, but the Spirit reinforces us as an army reinforces a beleaguered column. And he supplies the power we need for effective evangelism. We forfeit so much when we get out of step with him.

In these chapters, Paul points out the pitfalls, and charts a course that will guard us against grieving the Spirit. He sets up signposts that will help us to stay on the right road.

Reverence his person

First of all, *we must reverence his Person*. I confess that I cringe whenever I hear the Holy Spirit called 'It', for he is not a power or an influence. He is a Person. The word 'grieves' makes that clear, for we do not grieve a post box, we grieve a person. The Holy Spirit has all the marks of personality: he speaks, he prays, he teaches, he commands, he forbids, and so on.

A divine person

Paul says, 'Do not grieve the Holy Spirit of God', so he is a Divine Person. He shares life in the Godhead with the Father and the Son. He is *God* the Spirit. He is eternal, he is infinite, he is sovereign, and those are all the marks of Deity. So we should think about him with reverence. We should never call him 'It', for that is insulting. I would not want anybody to call my wife 'It'!

A loving person

And he is a loving person. 'Grieve' is a love word, and has deep feeling in it. Some Christians are frightened of the Holy Spirit, so they keep him at arm's length. Any mention of him alarms them, but how foolish for he loves us with a warm, tender love, and only wants the best for us.

In John 14:16–17, Jesus says to his disciples, 'And I will ask the Father, and he will give you another Counsellor to be with you for ever—the Spirit of truth.' The Greek word for 'another' means 'another of the same kind', and that illustrates the intensity of the Spirit's love for us. He has the same care and concern for us that the Lord Jesus had for his disciples. What a 'Counsellor' Jesus proved to be! He did so much for his disciples. He stood with them amidst all the shifting scenes of life. He was always there to give help and advice. And he came alongside them again and again to help them, like a boat bringing needed supplies.

The Holy Spirit has that kind of ministry in our lives today. He strengthens us. He gives us courage. He puts iron into our souls. He loves us, and wants to help us in every way possible, especially in dark and difficult days. He enables, he empowers, he encourages. He is always there to help, but he is no feather bed! He is rather steel in the backbone, equal to every circumstance and emergency of life.

How important not to grieve the Holy Spirit, for we need him at every turn of the road. So we must reverence his Person.

Remember his presence

As Paul charts the course that will keep us in step with the Spirit, we meet another helpful signpost. *We must remember his Presence.* Every born-again believer has the Holy Spirit. Romans 8:9 makes that crystal clear, for it says, 'If anyone does not have the Spirit of Christ, he does not belong to Christ.' So if we *do* belong to him, we *do* have the Holy Spirit! In 1 Corinthians 6:19, Paul says, 'Do you not know that your body is a temple of the Holy Spirit, who is in you, whom you have received from God?'

An elderly man gave his testimony at a certain conference. He said, 'I've loved the Saviour for years, but never until this week did I know that the Holy Spirit was living in me.' How sad! Do you know that the Holy Spirit is living in you?

If God has saved us, the Lord Jesus is not just beside us; by his Spirit he is living within us. A rector's wife went to a meeting at which this truth was explained. Afterwards she said to the speaker, 'I've been in the church all my life, but the vast difference between Jesus being *beside* us, and his being *in* us, had never occurred to me. I see it now! Light is breaking in all over!'

God's seal
Paul says, 'And do not grieve the Holy Spirit of God, with whom you were sealed for the day of redemption' (Ephesians 4:30). The moment God saves us we belong to him. We become *his* people, and he seals us with his Spirit.

Paul sent this letter to Ephesus, where the seal was in constant use. Ephesus had a busy port, and a constant stream of trade ebbed and flowed on the quayside. All kinds of things were bought and sold, and the seal proved very important. For example, a man bought twenty bags of corn, but he did not take them home with him. He left them on the quayside and sealed them with his own special seal. They were his the moment he bought them, but he sealed them to prove that he owned them. He would collect them later. Paul has that picture in mind when he says, 'And do not grieve the Holy Spirit of God, with whom you were sealed for the day of redemption.'

When God saves us, he seals us with his Spirit. He says, 'You're Mine! I've given you My Spirit to prove it.' So the sealing brings assurance. This ties in with Romans 8:16: 'The Spirit himself testifies with our spirit that we *are* God's children.' How careful we must be, then, not to grieve the Spirit, for grieving him will undermine our assurance. Remember his Presence!

The day of redemption
The merchant sealed his twenty bags of corn because he planned to take them home. And when God seals us with his Spirit he says, 'You must be delivered to my home.' What a fabulous future that suggests! God is a great God, so he must have a great home! The Lord Jesus said to his disciples, 'In my Father's house are many rooms; if it were not so, I would have told you. I am going there to prepare a place for you' (John 14:2). Every blood-bought believer is heading home!

The seal of God's Spirit guarantees that, for if he has started a work in our lives he will most certainly finish it. God writes no unfinished symphonies! That assurance undergirds Philippians 1:6. Paul says, I am 'confident of this, that he who began a good work in you *will* carry it on to completion until the day of Christ Jesus'.

So every true Christian is in transit for glory, what Paul calls in Ephesians 4:30: 'the day of redemption'. On that climactic day, God will put the finishing touches to his work in us. He will lay his perfecting hand on everything. We shall be perfect people, with not a trace of sin in our hearts. We shall have perfect bodies, with no trace of weakness, illness, or disease. And we shall enjoy perfect relationships in a perfect world. What a glorious prospect!

When God seals us with his Spirit, he seals us for that. So remember his Presence, and guard your relationship with him. Beware of grieving him, for we need the assurance he alone can give. The indwelling Holy Spirit can make heaven real to us, and give us anticipations of it, even before we get there! What a tonic for troubled hearts! And what an incentive to keep in step with him!

Regard his pleasure

As Paul charts the right course through these chapters, he moves very quickly into the realm of relationships. And we meet another signpost that points us to the right road. Paul describes the Spirit as 'the *Holy* Spirit of God', for he is so clean and pure. He hates sin, and recoils from it as a man recoils from a deadly snake. So *we must regard his Pleasure*—especially in our relationships.

As Paul exposes some of the things that grieve the Spirit, he begins with lying. He says, 'Therefore each of you must put off falsehood and speak truthfully to his neighbour'—and he tells us why—'for we are all members of one body' (Ephesians 4:25).

As we have seen already, church membership is body membership, not club membership. People gather in clubs because they have a common interest, but church membership is very different, for in Christ we have a common life. We belong to one another like members of a human body, so if we tell lies about others, or even about ourselves, we harm the Body life of the church. We betray the unity and trust that should knit our hearts in Christ.

Sins of the tongue

How important, then, that we trade in the truth, for our words can help or hinder our church life as we have seen already. They can enrich or degrade our relationships. In v. 29, Paul says, 'Do not let any unwholesome talk come out of your mouths, but only what is helpful for building others up according to their needs, that it may benefit those who listen.' Then he goes straight on to say, 'And do not grieve the Holy Spirit of God', which means that sins of the tongue certainly grieve him.

If we filtered all our words through v. 29, then everything we said would be helpful, edifying, and beneficial. Our fellow-believers would be glad to have us around! But sometimes anger boils up in our hearts, and our tongues run away with us. Our words pour out unfiltered, and they can do a great deal of damage. So in v. 26, Paul cautions us, 'In your anger do not sin'.

We find anger difficult to handle, but there *is* a righteous anger, an anger not soiled by selfishness. The Lord Jesus got angry at times, but never for himself, as we have seen already. He got angry when he saw others being hurt. Some of the things that happen in our world should make our blood boil, not because of their effect on us but because of their effect on others.

Paul says, 'In your anger do not sin: do not let the sun go down while you are still angry, and do not give the devil a foothold' (vv. 26–27). In v. 31, Paul links 'anger' with 'rage', which has been described as 'anger with the lid off'! Whatever form it takes deal with any anger in your heart before you go to bed, or you will take the devil into your bedroom, and you will not get a very good night's rest!

More sins of the tongue

In 5:4, Paul mentions some more sins of the tongue—'obscenity, foolish talk … coarse joking'—and again they involve others. These things, like muddy water, soil everything they touch, and should have no place in the Christian life. Paul tells us to replace them with 'thanksgiving', and what a different effect that has!

He is not forbidding good, clean fun. I believe the Lord Jesus had a sense of humour, and spoke sometimes with a twinkle in his eye. But humour can get out of hand, and Paul cautions us against that. We must never use our tongue to degrade others, or to drag them down. 'But rather thanksgiving', says Paul, for that will do so much good. It will encourage others, and lift them up.

Does the stream of thanksgiving, gratitude, and praise flow from *your* lips? Does it flow up to God, and does it flow out to others? Such a stream flowing out will refresh those around us, and make them feel good. The only time I heard from some members in the churches that I pastored, was when they had something to complain about. How sad! Be an encourager! Be quick to give thanks, and be slow to complain, for we can always find something to be thankful about, even on the darkest day.

Beware of bitterness

Paul says, 'And do not grieve the Holy Spirit of God, with whom you were sealed for the day of redemption.' Then, 'Get rid of all bitterness ...', for that certainly grieves him! Paul groups it with 'rage and anger, brawling and slander, along with every form of malice' (v. 31), for they all belong to the same family. What an unpleasant brood it is! And how they ruin our relationships!

The apostle begins with bitterness because it often spawns these things. He says, 'Get rid of *all* bitterness', every trace of it, for it can smoulder in our hearts for years. I have seen it happen. Maybe we were wronged in some way, or we were denied some honour or election, or we were slighted for some reason, either intentionally or unintentionally, and instead of yielding it to the Lord that *he* might deal with it, we brooded on it and became bitter.

One woman harboured bitterness and jealousy against a certain person for a long time—and the two things often go together. But at last she faced up to it. She brought the whole thing out before God in confession, and she said, 'I have a mental cancer!' She was right, and how it grieves the Holy Spirit!

Paul urges us to put it away, to drum it out of our lives, to refuse it shelter, to deny it board and lodging. For it saddens the Holy Spirit whose heart beats with love. It makes it impossible to keep in step with him. We *must* remember his presence!

How to resist

Again and again in these chapters, Paul shows us that the way to resist sin is to replace it, and I find that very helpful. He brings us to a fork in the road and he says, 'Go this way not that way.' He tells us to replace lying with the truth. He tells us to replace stealing with honest, useful work. He tells us to replace evil, unhelpful talk with thanksgiving. Paul sums up this approach in Romans 12 when he says, 'Do not be overcome by evil, but overcome evil with good' (v. 21).

A life of love

In Ephesians 4:32, Paul tells us to replace bitterness and its ugly brood with love. He says, 'Be kind and compassionate to one another, forgiving each other, just as in Christ God forgave you.' Love belongs to a very different family, and Paul describes it in all its attractiveness. In 5:1–2, he says, 'Be imitators of God, therefore, as dearly loved children and live a life of love, just as Christ loved us and gave himself for us as a fragrant offering and sacrifice to God.'

What great love! With two telling phrases, Paul hangs up a picture of it, that we might see it in all its splendour, for he wants to make it vivid and real. So he says, 'just as … God', and 'just as Christ'. Here is our pattern. If God has saved us we see it demonstrated in our own lives, for how wonderfully God has loved *us!* Paul describes us as 'dearly loved children'. He says, 'Christ loved *us* and gave himself for *us*'. Now we are to be the channels of this love to others. We are to show this same love in *our* relationships.

Paul says, 'Be imitators of God, therefore, as dearly loved children'. For 'imitators' Paul uses the Greek word *mimetes,* from which we get our words 'mimic' and 'mimicry'. What great mimics the children are! One day I walked about with my hands behind my back, and I turned round to see my little granddaughter walking in exactly the same way! If we are God's children we are to mimic *him*. I like Eugene Petersen's paraphrase: 'Keep company with him and learn a life of love.'

God's love in Christ has a delightful fragrance about it, a fragrance that rises supremely from the Cross of Calvary. For Paul says, 'Christ loved us and gave himself up for us as a fragrant offering and sacrifice to God'. What an incentive to open our lives to God daily, to spend time with him in Bible study and prayer! For if we do, something, *something* of the fragrance of his love will cling to us.

I remember visiting a perfume factory in Paris. My wife and I spent some time in its scented atmosphere, seeing how the different perfumes were made. When we came out on to the busy Paris street, and boarded the coach that stood waiting for us, the fragrance still clung to us! And it scented the atmosphere for some time afterwards! I want to carry the fragrance of God's love wherever I go. May that be your desire too.

Rely on his power

As Paul continues to chart the course that will keep us in step with the Spirit, we meet one more signpost that will help us to stay on the right road. *We must rely on his Power*. In 4:30, Paul turns from the negative, 'Do not grieve the Holy Spirit of God', to the positive, in 5:18, 'Be filled with the Spirit'. We must live in submissive partnership with the Holy Spirit, for we need his help not to grieve him.

The defeat of sin

We need his power to defeat sin, not least in our relationships. For we battle daily against the world, the flesh, and the devil. We face the world that is outside us, the flesh that is inside us, and the devil who knows how to exploit both for his own evil ends. He prowls around like a hungry lion looking for prey! And what an unholy trio they make! Left to ourselves we shall crash to defeat again and again. But God has not left us to ourselves. He has given us his Spirit, and he makes a powerful ally whenever we face temptation. He throws himself into our defence.

We find a vital key to victory in Romans 8:13 and I want to underscore it because it is so important. Paul says, 'For if you live according to the sinful nature, you will die; but if *by the Spirit* you put to death the misdeeds of the body, you will live'. The Christian life has been described as 'A personal partnership with the Provider of power.' What potential for holiness that suggests!

When temptation comes, and we cry to the Lord for help, he can give us immediate aid, for he lives within us by his Spirit. He could not be closer! In Psalm 25:15, David says, 'My eyes are ever on the Lord, for only *he* will release my feet from the snare.' The snare of temptation! When your feet get entangled, eyes off the snare, eyes off your feet, and eyes on the Lord! Cry to *him* for help! Keep looking to *him*.

Serving God

When we read the Acts of the Apostles we soon discover the power source of the church. We get our first clue in the words of Jesus in 1:8—'You will receive power when the Holy Spirit comes on you'. We get our second clue in 2:2—'Suddenly a sound like the blowing of a violent wind came from heaven'. The church has no power source on earth. We must look to heaven, to God's gift of his Spirit, for all the demands of service. We must beware of a proud independence of the Holy Spirit, for that grieves him, and robs us of the very power we need.

The early church was not a perfect church; it had faults and failings, and problems with relationships, just like the church today. But when things went wrong it dealt with them straightaway. And it was a powerful church because it worked in partnership with the Holy Spirit. It was powerful in evangelism because it relied on *his* power. And we need the Holy Spirit's power for *our* evangelism, whether it is public or personal.

A final word

'And do not grieve the Holy Spirit of God,' says Paul, 'with whom you were sealed for the day of redemption.' How important that we heed this vital verse. Paul has charted the right course for us, but we must follow it. He has set up the right signposts for us, but we must follow their directions.

We *must* guard our relationship with the Holy Spirit. We must reverence his Person. We must remember his Presence. We must regard his Pleasure. And we must rely on his Power. And that means, amongst other things, guarding our relationships with others.

Love's fruitfulness

Again and again, as we have explored the varied landscape of relationships, we have seen the difference that love makes. It bathes our lives with warmth and brightness like the sun shining on a clear day. And it lays its hand on *all* our relationships. It safeguards good relationships, strengthens threatened relationships, and salvages broken relationships.

John Blanchard, in a sermon on this theme, helps us to see this love in action. He tells us how it shows itself. He says, 'Whatever a person is, or does, or says, you will act, and speak, and think, as far as that person is concerned, with the deliberate intention of bringing about their highest good, and their greatest blessing.' It is undeniably the key to enduring, enriching and encouraging relationships, for it deals a death blow to the innate selfishness that troubles all of us.

We have seen how this love guards us from misunderstanding which can cause such havoc amongst God's people. It curbs the wrong kind of criticism that can be so destructive and so discouraging. It rescues us from bitterness and grievances that can warp our attitudes. And it helps us to show a forgiving spirit. Yes, what a difference love makes! It may be intolerant at times but only in the defence of others. It filters our words so that our lips drip honey and even salt, but not poison. We want to build others up and not drag them down, for love makes us aware of *their* needs not just our own. In both the church and the home it brings harmony and peace. We have seen what can happen when love breaks down.

But this love does not grow naturally in the human heart, for the weeds of selfishness can so easily choke it. We are all capable of love, but even the best human love has this core of selfishness. The love that the New Testament refers to is not natural, but supernatural. Paul describes it in Galatians 5 as 'the fruit of the Spirit' (v. 22). It has to be imported from the heart of God, and brought to us by the Holy Spirit. We see it demonstrated supremely in our Lord Jesus Christ, and especially at the cross. He is love's visual aid, so we must keep his life before us continually.

The factory of the flesh

Paul sets this love in contrast to 'the works of the flesh' (KJV), or 'the acts of the sinful nature' (v. 19). And from what Paul says we can picture it as a factory where all sorts of evil things are being manufactured. They pour off the assembly line in all their foulness, things like 'sexual immorality, impurity and debauchery; idolatry and witchcraft'. These things certainly touch the lives of others, but the things that follow, create havoc in our relationships. For Paul lists 'hatred, discord, jealousy, fits of rage, selfish ambition, dissensions, factions and envy; drunkenness, orgies, and the like' (vv. 19–21). This factory is managed by the old self, what Paul calls 'the flesh', or 'the sinful nature'. It has been described as 'a root of sinful self-interest'. And when it gets the upper hand these are the sort of things it produces from this hidden factory in our hearts.

Is it possible to put it out of business? It will not be easy, for the manager is very hostile to the Lord Jesus, and he will do his best to keep it in production. This sets up a conflict that no Christian can escape. Paul describes it in v. 17. He says, 'For the sinful nature desires what is contrary to the Spirit, and the Spirit what is contrary to the sinful nature' (v. 17). So conflict becomes inevitable, but Paul shows us how production in this factory can be slowed down, even if it cannot be halted altogether. He says, 'Live by the Spirit, and you will not gratify the desires of the sinful nature' (v. 16).

This marks out clearly the path of victory. If Jesus Christ lives in our hearts by his Spirit we *can* get the better of this foul factory manager. For we can resist him in the name of Jesus, and the very mention of the Lord's name helps us. And we can take a resolute stand against the things that spoil and soil our lives. We can say 'No!' to them firmly and repeatedly. That will cut down this factory's production! But we cannot do it on our own. We must yield ourselves unreservedly and unremittingly to the Lord Jesus, and live in daily partnership with him. All this is wrapped up in the words, 'Live by the Spirit'.

The orchard of the Spirit

With the word 'But' in v. 22, a very different picture emerges. We are no longer in a factory with all its evil production lines; we are in an orchard where the loveliest fruit grows. For Paul wants to show us what happens when we 'live by the Spirit'. The contrast could not be greater!

Paul says, 'The fruit of the Spirit is love, joy, peace, patience, kindness, goodness, faithfulness, gentleness and self-control' (vv. 22–23). But why does he say, 'The fruit of the Spirit *is*', and then list nine words? Has he forgotten the rules of grammar? Should it not have been, 'The *fruits* of the Spirit *are?*'

I like the way that G. Campbell Morgan explains it in one of his sermons in *The Westminster Pulpit*. He suggests that: 'love is the all-inclusive word, and the words that follow break it up and explain its meaning'. He says, 'If you have love you have all these things. If you lack love you lack them all'. This ties in with what Paul says in v. 14: 'The entire law is summed up in a single command: "Love your neighbour as yourself".' That makes love supreme. The Christian life is a life mastered and driven by love.

So when Paul says, 'The fruit of the Spirit is love', he has something big in mind. He breaks it up because he does not want us to devalue it. He does not want us to treat it as merely a sentimental word. We could think of it as one fruit with different flavours. This underscores its uniqueness, for no natural fruit would have such an impressive variety of flavours.

The attractive flavour of joy

Paul begins with *the attractive flavour of joy*. He says, 'The fruit of the Spirit is love—*joy*'. And the word means gladness, cheerfulness, and delight. And like the sun breaking through a bank of dark clouds, it can light up our lives even on the gloomiest day, for it is not dependent on circumstances, as we see in John 15:11. The Lord Jesus was but hours away from his arrest, his trial, and his crucifixion, yet he talks about 'my joy'. And we see it in Philippians 2:2. The apostle Paul was being kept under guard in Rome, chained to a Roman soldier, yet he too could speak about 'my joy'.

I had the privilege one day of meeting Richard Wurmbrand, the Romanian preacher, who suffered so grievously at the hands of the Communists. He spent fourteen years in prison, three of them in solitary confinement. In his book *In Search of God* he writes, 'The Communists believe that happiness comes from material satisfaction, but alone in my cell, cold, hungry and in rags, I danced for joy every night ... Sometimes I was so filled with joy that I felt I would burst if I did not give it expression.' Here was the joy that only God can give. Here was joy at its best with circumstances at their worst.

But the Christian's joy is no mere superficial exuberance. It may be dimmed at times from the outward eye by the hard knocks of life, but it keeps on bubbling up in the deep places of the heart. It is like a fresh-water spring by the seashore. Twice every day the salt tides roll over it, but the spring keeps on flowing, and when the brackish waters have rolled back, the water is as fresh as ever.

But what is it that keeps a man or a woman cheerful amidst the problems and difficulties of life? Nothing but love. See how the Lord Jesus ties love and joy together in John 15. He says, 'Remain in my love ... so that my joy may be in you and that your joy may be complete' (vv. 10–11). It is love that flavours our lives with joy. Human love can bring us a measure of joy, but it depends on what happens to us. How different from the joy that lit up Richard Wurmbrand's prison cell! That came from the assurance of *God's* love. Whatever happened he still had God, and God is faithful.

The mellow flavour of peace

Paul moves on to *the mellow flavour of peace*. He says, 'The fruit of the Spirit is love—joy, *peace*'. The cry for peace echoes around the world, for so many people are caught up in strife, discord, and disharmony. Day after day, conflicts of one kind and another hit the headlines. There are so many trouble spots where people are at one another's throats. But what makes peace so hard to find? Why is it so elusive? It is because we fail to look for it in the right place.

The Bible alone tracks it to its source. It begins when God turns enemies into friends, and pours *his* peace into their lives. And peace is very dear to God's heart. He is 'the God of peace' (Philippians 4:9). His Son is the 'Prince of peace' (Isaiah 9:6). His gospel is 'the gospel of peace' (Ephesians 6:15). Luke 1:79 tells us that God's Son, the Lord Jesus Christ, came 'to guide our feet into the path of peace.' And Colossians 1:20 shows us how much that cost him. It says that he made peace 'through his blood, shed on the cross'. Paul sums it up perfectly in Romans 5:1: 'Therefore, since we have been justified through faith, we have peace with God through our Lord Jesus Christ'.

So peace comes from a right relationship with God, from clinging to Jesus Christ as our Lord and Saviour, from trusting and following him. He himself said, 'Peace I leave with you; my peace I give you ... do not let your hearts be troubled and do not be afraid' (John 14:27). As this peace ripples through our hearts it releases us from friction and fear. Then it ripples out into our relationships. We are able to obey Romans 12:18: 'If it is possible, as far as it depends on you, live at peace with everyone.'

All this helps us to unpack the peace imparted by the Holy Spirit. It is not the peace of the cemetery, but the peace that follows conflict. Opposing forces have been harmonised, and fellowship has been restored, but what can produce such peace? Nothing but love. It is love that flavours our lives with peace. To live at peace we must learn to love. That is the key to harmonious relationships in the home, the church, and the community.

The strong flavour of patience

Paul moves next to *the strong flavour of patience*. He says, 'The fruit of the Spirit is love—joy, peace, *patience*'. The Greek word has two parts to it. The first part, *makro*, means long or far. The second part, *thumos*, means anger. So *makrothumia* puts anger a long way off, it keeps it at a distance. It has a long fuse. It may burn through eventually, but it takes a long time.

God has this 'patience' or he would have wiped this world out ages ago. He does get angry, and God's anger is a terrible thing, but he is 'slow to anger' (Psalm 103:8). He has a great wealth of patience, Romans 2:4, which keeps his anger in check. Patience has been described as 'a virtue that carries a lot of wait!'

And how much *we* need this patience, for life can throw up many things that irritate us and put us in a bad mood. We can become impatient with the ways of God. A spirit of impatience can creep into our prayer life when life gets tough and God fails to answer our prayers. And the state of the world can make us impatient. We say, 'When is the Lord coming again to sort things out?'

James tackles this impatient spirit head-on when he says, 'Be patient, then, brothers, until the Lord's coming. See how the farmer waits for the land to yield its valuable crop and how patient he is for the autumn and spring rains. You too, be patient and stand firm, because the Lord's coming is near. Don't grumble …' (4:7–9).

And we can become impatient with the ways of men, especially if we have a short fuse! So many things can upset us, from traffic jams to delayed flights, from disobedient children to a nagging spouse, from hospital waiting lists to too much red tape. And impatience can trigger road rage, trolley rage, and even air rage! People cannot control their temper and they let rip! What will keep us patient amidst all the provocations of life? Nothing but love! Paul says plainly 'Love is patient' (1 Corinthians 13:4), and he uses this same Greek word, *makrothumia*. It is love that flavours our lives with patience. Someone has described patience as 'concentrated strength', and love gives us the strength we need to keep our temper and tongue in check. We shall be able to provide the 'gentle answer' that 'turns away wrath' (Proverbs 15:1). I have seen more than one explosive situation defused in that way.

The disciples provoked the Lord Jesus again and again; yet how patient he was with them. They were so slow to grasp the truth. They were over-protective of Jesus, so they tried to turn children and their parents away from him, and they wanted to call down fire on a village that would not receive him. And they were so eager for status in the Lord's kingdom, and that sparked a jealous quarrel amongst them.

Yet the Lord went on training them because he loved them. He never lost his temper with them. In John 13, Jesus is moving inexorably to the cross, and v. 1 says, 'Having loved his own who were in the world, he now showed them the full extent of his love.' And if we share his love we shall share his patience too.

The lovely flavour of kindness

Paul turns next to *the lovely flavour of kindness*. He says, 'The fruit of the Spirit is love—joy, peace, patience, *kindness*'. How wonderfully kind God has been to us! Ephesians 2:7 refers to 'his kindness to us in Christ Jesus', so the river of God's kindness laps the shore of every believer's life. How kind we should be then to one another! As Colossians 3:12 puts it, 'As God's chosen people … clothe yourselves with … kindness'. Make it as obvious in your life as the clothes you put on, for a kind father wants kind children. He wants kindness to be one of the hallmarks of his family.

And what a difference it makes! Kindness speaks an international language that needs no translation. It rescues life from coldness and selfishness, and makes it warm and interesting. It gives our faith hands and feet. It makes us aware of others and alert to their needs, especially in the small things of life. In Matthew 10:42, Jesus said that even 'a cup of cold water' given as an act of kindness counts in heaven. So 'Be kind … to one another' (Ephesians 4:32). Look for ways of being helpful. Opportunities for kindness abound everywhere if we have the eyes to see them and the heart to seize them.

But what makes us really kind? Nothing but love. 1 Corinthians 13:4 says simply, 'love is kind'. Charles Swindoll, in his book *Simple Faith*, says, 'Love has been called the most effective motivational force in all the world. When love is at work in us, it is remarkable how giving and forgiving, understanding and tolerant we can be.' Yes, and how kind too!

How beautifully the Lord Jesus, who was Incarnate Love, mirrored kindness in his life! He was so alert to the needs of others, and he was constantly reaching out to help them. And love will flavour our lives with kindness too.

The striking flavour of goodness

Paul continues with *the striking flavour of goodness*. He says, 'The fruit of the Spirit is love—joy, peace, patience, kindness, *goodness*'. The world does not always report goodness enthusiastically. It sometimes hammers the 'do-gooders' because they fail to make goodness attractive in their own lives. We can sympathise with the little girl who prayed, 'Lord, make the bad people good, and Lord, please make the good people nice!'

Barnabas reflected that kind of goodness, and Acts 11:24 gives us his secret. It says, 'He was a good man, full of the Holy Spirit and faith'. His goodness was not self-made. It came from knowing Jesus Christ and sharing his life with him, and that kind of goodness is always attractive.

We see it perfectly in the Lord Jesus himself, in a portrait that the apostle Peter painted in the home of Cornelius, the Roman centurion. Peter produced it with a few deft strokes of his verbal brush as the people listened hungrily to his words. He said, 'God anointed Jesus of Nazareth with the Holy Spirit and power, and ... he went around doing good and healing all who were under the power of the devil, because God was with him' (Acts 10:38). The Lord Jesus certainly made goodness attractive! His severest critics cannot dispute that.

And God wants to see this goodness in his people. Petersen has a helpful paraphrase of Titus 2:14: 'Jesus Christ ... offered himself as a sacrifice to free us from a dark, rebellious life into this good, pure life, making us a people he can be proud of, energetic in goodness.' I like that. Energetic in goodness! Cecil Alexander took up this theme in the hymn: 'There is a green hill far away'. In the second verse she wrote, 'He died that we might be forgiven, he died to make us *good*.'

But what inspires this goodness? Nothing but love. What a squall of temptation Joseph faced when he served as a slave in Egypt! Potiphar's wife tried to tempt him into her bed, and she was very persistent. But he said, 'My master has withheld nothing from me except you, because you are his wife. How then could I do such a wicked thing and sin against God?' (Genesis 39:9). We find the same inspiration of goodness in John 14:15. Jesus said, 'If you *love* me, you will obey what I command.' G. Campbell Morgan says, 'That is the whole philosophy of goodness.' Yes it is love that flavours our lives with goodness.

The distinctive flavour of faithfulness

Paul comes next to *the distinctive flavour of faithfulness*. He says, 'The fruit of the Spirit is love—joy, peace, patience, kindness, goodness, *faithfulness*'. In a world besmirched with unfaithfulness, this virtue shines out like a beacon on a dark night. Broken promises litter the earth. Commitments collapse because too many people prove unfaithful. They break their word as easily as they give it. The Divorce Courts provide sad testimony to that. And what disillusionment King Solomon reveals when he says, 'Many a man claims to have unfailing love, but a faithful man who can find?' (Proverbs 20:6).

But how wonderfully faithful God is! He not only saves us, he keeps us. We can trust him in every situation. He says, 'Never will I leave you; never will I forsake you' (Hebrews 13:5). What a well of assurance that is! We can draw buckets of confidence from it, for God never breaks a promise. And he wants us to be faithful too, faithful to him and faithful to one another.

Our word should be our bond. Our family, our church, our friends, our business associates, should be able to rely on us. If we make promises we should do our best to keep them. But what inspires faithfulness? What will keep us faithful amidst all the vagaries of life? Nothing but love. It is love that flavours our lives with faithfulness.

A couple whose marriage is rooted in the soil of love will never be unfaithful to each other. Their love will keep them together through thick and thin, for true love always has loyalty in it. They will be there for each other whatever tests and troubles they face. We find this same faithfulness in Jesus' love for his disciples, for he stood by them right to the end. Where love acts as a sentry we shall never desert the post of duty. Love will keep us faithful.

The sweet flavour of gentleness

Paul continues with *the sweet flavour of gentleness*. He says, 'The fruit of the Spirit is love—joy, peace, patience, kindness, goodness, faithfulness, *gentleness*'. We find this word twinned with humility, which shows us what sort of family it belongs to. The Lord Jesus said, 'Take my yoke upon you and learn from me, for I am gentle and humble in heart, and you will find rest for your souls' (Matthew 11:29). And Ephesians 4:2 says, 'Be completely humble and gentle'.

The Greek word for 'gentle' is *praus*. It is difficult to translate but clearly it has no pride or arrogance in it. It leaves no room for self-assertion. Like the Lord Jesus it can receive injury without resentment, and praise without conceit. It was used of an animal that has been tamed, and that throws light on it. A wild horse, for example, is broken in and becomes obedient to the bit and the bridle. That horse is *praus*.

So 'gentleness' is not weakness; there is nothing spineless about it. It does not rule out anger, for the Lord Jesus got angry at times, but it is anger kept on a leash. It has the strength of steel in it but its strength has been brought under control. John the Baptist fleshed it out when he said of Jesus, 'He must become greater; I must become less' (John 3:30). He pushed Jesus forward and took a back seat himself.

'Gentleness' keeps self in the place of submission. It lives under God's mastery. What is the secret of it? Nothing but love. It is love that flavours our lives with gentleness. It is love that makes us reasonable without becoming weak, and submissive without becoming spineless.

The mature flavour of self-control

Paul turns finally to *the mature flavour of self-control*. He says, 'The fruit of the Spirit is love—joy, peace, patience, kindness, goodness, faithfulness, gentleness and *self-control'*. We have seen already what a problem we can have with the old self, for it wants to clamber back on to the throne of our hearts and run our lives. It wants to take the flag of Jesus down and run up its own flag. So we *must* exercise 'self-control', which suggests a balanced, disciplined life. We must keep ourselves well in hand, and Proverbs 16:32 encourages that, for it says, 'Better ... a man who controls his temper than one who takes a city.'

This 'self-control' brings these verses to a great climax because without it 'the fruit of the Spirit' with all its different flavours, will not appear in our lives. The old self will nip off its buds before they have an opportunity to grow. We must yield ourselves unreservedly to the Lord Jesus each new day so that his Spirit can control our lives.

What tremendous self-control Jesus exercised! He faced some dreadful provocations at Calvary, but 1 Peter 2:23 says, 'When they hurled their insults at him, he did not retaliate; when he suffered, he made no threats. Instead, he entrusted himself to him who judges justly.' And in that marvellous pen portrait of Jesus in Isaiah 53, it says, 'He was oppressed and afflicted, yet he did not open his mouth; he was led like a lamb to the slaughter, and as a sheep before her shearers is silent, so he did not open his mouth' (v. 7). What incredible self-control! And we should 'follow in his steps' (1 Peter 2:21), like following footsteps in the sand.

But what will motivate this 'self-control'? Nothing but love. It has been described as 'the victory of love'. That is what motivated it in the life of the Lord Jesus. He was love-mastered and love-driven. And it is love that will flavour our lives with self-control.

Fruit suggests cultivation

'The fruit of the Spirit' then 'is love', and the things that follow are different